Essential G

O. M. Thomson

1978

Oxford University Press

Oxford University Press, Walton Street, Oxford OX2 6DP

Oxford London Glasgow
New York Toronto Melbourne Wellington
Ibadan Nairobi Dar Es Salaam Cape Town
Kuala Lumpur Singapore Jakarta Hong Kong Tokyo
Delhi Bombay Calcutta Madras Karachi

ISBN 019 831130 3

© O. M. Thomson 1978

First published 1978
Reprinted 1978

Printed in Great Britain by offset lithography by
Billing & Sons Ltd, Guildford, London and Worcester

Foreword

What's the use of grammar? A knowledge of it is part of the technique of writing. For a good writer understands the character of words and the way they are formed; he knows how to write well-shaped sentences that read clearly and end firmly; and his writing has economy, and it's lucid, because he knows how to re-arrange his words so as to get rid of hitches and ambiguities and awkward repetitions. It's not easy to learn to write like that if you don't know how the language works.

> *True ease in writing comes from art, not chance,*
> *As those move easiest who have learned to dance . . .*

— it's an old truth, and there's no way of dodging it.

How much grammar does a student need to know? What aspects of it will help him with his writing? How much is fussy academic detail, which will only confuse him and discourage him? In this book I have included only those points which I think he needs to understand, and I have tried to explain them in such a way that he becomes aware of the usefulness of what he is learning.

O. M. Thomson

Contents

Different kinds of words
George Orwell: *A Hanging*

Verbs
Cecil Woodham-Smith: *The Charge of the Light Brigade*

Nouns and Verbs
D. H. Lawrence: *The Rainbow*

Sentences
Nevil Shute: *A Town Like Alice*

Different kinds of words

Extracts taken from

George Orwell:
A Hanging

1 Nouns

A noun is a name. It may be the name of a person, like *Sarah,* or of a place, like *London.* If it is a noun of this kind, beginning with a capital letter, it is called a proper noun.

Or it may be the name of something we can touch or see, like *a star,* or *the desk. Star* and *desk* are concrete nouns.

We can also name things that we can't touch or see – things which have no physical reality – like *truth, honour, happiness.* These are abstract nouns.

There is another kind: collective nouns. They are names of groups, like *crowd, committee, team.*

George Orwell, who served in the Imperial Police during the 1920s, wrote an account of a hanging he witnessed:

It was in Burma, a sodden morning of the rains. A sickly light, like yellow tinfoil, was slanting over the high walls into the jail yard. We were waiting outside the condemned cells, a row of sheds fronted with double bars, like small animal cages. Each cell measured about ten feet by ten and was quite bare within except for a plank bed and a pot for drinking water. In some of them brown, silent men were squatting at the inner bars, with their blankets draped round them. These were the condemned men, due to be hanged within the next week or two.

---

1   Orwell names three things that were to be found inside the cells. What were they?

2   What kind of nouns are the three you have just written down?

3   Read again the last three sentences in the paragraph; then, in three sentences of your own, describe a cell in an English prison. Underline the concrete nouns you use.

4   What kind of noun is *Burma?*

5   Write down the names of three prisons in England. What kind of nouns are they?

6   Try to imagine what the feelings of those condemned men might have been as they waited in that prison in Burma. Try to think of three different kinds of feeling, and write down the three nouns that name them. What kind of nouns are they?

7   Write two or three sentences about the condemned men, or about just one of them, introducing the three nouns you thought of for question 6.

8   *A gang of about twenty-five prisoners were being led across the yard.* What kind of noun is *gang?* Notice that we can write *were* after a noun of this kind, even though it is in the singular.

9   Now make up a sentence with a collective noun in it – one that isn't mentioned on either of these two pages.

10   Most nouns form their plural by adding an *s* ending. But not all do. There are two in Orwell's paragraph that don't. Which are they?

11   *Rains,* in the first sentence, is an unusual word, since we nearly always use this noun in its singular form. Explain the difference between *rain* and *the rains.*

3

2 Adjectives

Adjectives describe nouns. To put it more exactly, they modify them by adding to their meaning. Orwell described those condemned prisoners as *brown, silent men:* by choosing different adjectives we can turn them into *fat, jocular men.*

The imaginative power that adjectives have should never be squandered. It will be, if you use too many or choose them thoughtlessly. Orwell chooses his with care. Do you remember how he described the morning and the light? Don't turn the page back. His description, with blanks for the two adjectives he used, went like this:

It was in Burma, a —— morning of the rains. A —— light, like yellow tinfoil, was slanting over the high walls into the jail yard.

Write out those sentences with the two blanks filled in. Probably you won't remember the adjectives Orwell used; so put in two of your own, making the morning as wet as you can and the light as unpleasant as possible. Then turn back the page and compare your adjectives with his.

One prisoner had been brought out of his cell. He was a Hindu, a puny wisp of a man, with a shaven head and vague liquid eyes. He had a thick, sprouting moustache, absurdly too big for his body, rather like the moustache of a comic man on the films. Six tall Indian warders were guarding him and getting him ready for the gallows.

Eight o'clock struck and a bugle call, desolately thin in the wet air, floated from the distant barracks. The superintendent of the jail, who was standing apart from the rest of us, moodily prodding the gravel with his stick, raised his head at the sound. He was an army doctor, with a grey toothbrush moustache and a gruff voice. 'For God's sake hurry up, Francis,' he said irritably. 'The man ought to have been dead by this time. Aren't you ready yet?'

Francis, the head jailer, a fat Dravidian in a white drill suit and gold spectacles, waved his black hand. 'Yes sir, yes sir,' he bubbled. 'All iss satisfactorily prepared. The hangman iss waiting.'

---

1 In the second and third sentences of that passage Orwell describes
   the prisoner. Write down all the adjectives he uses. Don't include
   sprouting, because it's part of a verb.

2 Orwell doesn't tell us anything about the six Indian warders
   except that they were tall. Try to picture one of them, and
   describe him in two or three sentences. Then underline the
   adjectives you used.

3 What noun does *big* (in line 4) modify? And what one does *thin*
   modify (in line 7)?

4 A noun can be placed in front of another noun in order to modify
   it, in the same way as an adjective can be: *a prison warder, a world
   war, the death penalty*. Are there any nouns in the extract which are
   used in this way? Write down as many as you can find.

5 Many adjectives can be changed into nouns by having -*ness* added
   to them. *Sweet, sweetness*. How many in the quoted passage can
   be? Write them down as nouns. A group of letters which is added
   to the end of a word, like -*ness*, is called a suffix.

6 If we add *un*- to the beginning of a word it usually changes its
   meaning into the opposite. Two adjectives in the extract can be
   changed in this way. Write them down with the *un*- added to
   them. A group of letters added to the beginning of a word is
   called a prefix.

7 Write down the adjective that means the opposite of *liquid* (line 3);
   and then the one that means the opposite of *wet* (line 8).

8 How do *liquid* and *wet* differ in meaning? This is a very difficult
   difference to explain. Think of the two opposites you have just
   written down: that will help you.

9 Orwell doesn't tell us what lay between the prison and the distant
   barracks. Perhaps it was some kind of swamp? Perhaps there was
   a road? Perhaps some people were working there? Try to picture
   the scene, and describe it in not more than fifty words, putting in
   as many small details as you can.

10 Choose a descriptive passage about ten lines long, from a book or
   a newspaper, and copy it out leaving blanks for all the adjectives
   which make the description effective. Then hand it to your
   neighbour for him to fill in the blanks with adjectives of his own
   choice.

3 Adverbs, used with verbs

Adverbs modify the meanings of verbs. Adverbs of manner tell us *how* somebody did something: *He spoke rudely.* Adverbs of time tell us *when: He arrived early.* Adverbs of place tell us *where: He waited there.*

Adverbs of manner have the same kind of imaginative power that adjectives have. Often they enrich the meaning. Do you remember how the superintendent prodded the ground with his stick? He prodded it 'moodily'. By choosing a different adverb we could make him prod it *playfully*, or *furiously*. And do you remember how he spoke to Francis. He was tensed up. *'For God's sake hurry up, Francis,' he said* ———.

What adverb would come in well there? Put one in, writing the sentence out in full, and then turn back to page 4 to see what Orwell used.

The condemned man was handcuffed and his arms were lashed to his sides:

We set out for the gallows. Two warders marched on either side of the prisoner, with their rifles at the slope; two others marched close against him, gripping him by arm and shoulder, as though at once pushing and supporting him. The rest of us, magistrates and the like, followed behind. Suddenly, when we had gone ten yards, the procession stopped short without any order or warning. A dreadful thing had happened – a dog, come goodness knows whence, had appeared in the yard. It came bounding among us with a loud volley of barks and leapt round us wagging its whole body, wild with glee at finding so many human beings together. It was a large woolly dog, half Airedale, half pariah. For a moment it pranced round us, and then, before anyone could stop it, it had made a dash for the prisoner, and jumping up tried to lick his face. Everybody stood aghast, too taken aback even to grab the dog.

'Who let that bloody brute in here?' said the superintendent angrily. 'Catch it, someone!'

A warder, detached from the escort, charged clumsily after the dog.

---

1 What verb does *suddenly,* in line 6, modify?

2 Write down two adverbs of manner that come in the last four lines of the extract, and after each one write down the verb it modifies.

3 What adverb could be fitted into the passage, as an extra, to modify *gripping* (line 3)? And can you think of another one that could be fitted in to modify *pranced* (line 13)?

4 There are several adjectives in the passage that can be changed into adverbs by having the suffix *-ly* added to them. Write down as many as you can find, and use them as adverbs in sentences of your own.

5 What kind of noun is *glee,* in line 11? By adding a suffix to it turn it into an adjective. Then, by adding a second suffix, turn it into an adverb.

6 What kind of noun is *brute,* in the fourth line from the end? Turn it first into an adjective by adding one suffix. Then, by adding another one, turn it into an adverb. Finally, by adding a different suffix to the adjective, turn it into an abstract noun.

7 By altering its last two letters turn *magistrate* (line 5) into an abstract noun. You may need the help of a dictionary.

8 Will you now turn back to page 4 and look at the second paragraph of the extract. First write down all the adjectives and adverbs which are used in connection with the superintendent, and after each word you write put either *adj.* or *adv.* . . . .

9 . . . Then, drawing your conclusions from those words, describe his character, in three or four lines.

10 Orwell's procession was making for the gallows. Think of three other kinds of processions, or marches; name them; and after each one write down an adverb showing how the people taking part would be likely to walk or march.

4 Adverbs, used with adjectives and other adverbs

Adverbs can also modify adjectives: *extremely slow, very sad, too quiet.* And they can modify other adverbs: *extremely slowly, very sadly, too quietly. Extremely, very,* and *too* are called adverbs of degree, because they answer the question, *to what extent?* There are several more: *almost, completely, rather . . .*

Orwell tells us that the bugle call which came from the distant barracks sounded

—— *thin in the wet air.*

Do you remember what adverb he used to modify *thin?* It wasn't anything as obvious as *extremely,* or *very.* In fact it wasn't an adverb of degree at all, but one of manner, telling us *in what way* the bugle call sounded thin. Write down an adverb of manner that you think would do well, and then turn back to page 4 and see what Orwell put.

It was several minutes before someone managed to catch the dog. Then we put my handkerchief through its collar and moved off once more, with the dog still straining and whimpering.

It was about forty yards to the gallows. I watched the bare brown back of the prisoner marching in front of me. He walked clumsily with his bound arms, but quite steadily, with that bobbing gait of the Indian who never straightens his knees. At each step his muscles slid neatly into place, the lock of hair on his scalp danced up and down, his feet printed themselves on the wet gravel. And once, in spite of the men who gripped him by each shoulder, he stepped slightly aside to avoid a puddle on the path.

---

1 There are two adverbs in that extract which are themselves modified by adverbs. That makes two pairs. Write down each pair.

2 Look at the first pair. What kind of adverb is the first one of the two – is it one of manner, time, place, or degree? And what kind is the second one?

3 Look at the second pair. What kind is the first adverb? And the second one?

4 Will you now turn back to page 4. In the first paragraph of the extract there is an adjective that is modified by an adverb, and this adverb is in turn modified by another one. Write down the three words. What kind of adverb is the first one of the two? And what kind is the second one?

5 *It was several minutes before someone managed to catch the dog.* What do you imagine happened during those minutes? Did the superintendent join in the chase? Or the other warders? Or the fat Francis, in his white drill suit and gold spectacles? What was the prisoner doing? Describe what you think might have happened, in a paragraph of four or five lines. Introduce some adverbs of manner, which are useful words for showing how people move.

6 Orwell tells us that the man walked *clumsily* but *quite steadily.* In one or two sentences of your own, and using at least two adverbs, describe a quite different sort of man walking in a quite different way. Underline the adverbs you used.

7 What is the force of the adverb *neatly,* as Orwell uses it in the second paragraph? Does it just have its obvious visual effect, enabling us to picture the movement of the prisoner's muscles? Or – in view of the grim circumstances – does it also bring to mind some other thoughts? If so, *what* thoughts? And why does it bring them to mind?

8 Find a short passage, in a book or a newspaper, which contains at least two adverbs of manner. Copy it out, leaving blanks for them, and then hand it to your neighbour for him to fill in the blanks with adverbs of his own choice.

5 Words that can be used as both adjectives and adverbs

Adverbs, then, modify verbs, adjectives, and other adverbs. They can never modify nouns. Only adjectives can. Nobody talks about a slowly train, or a soon train, or an often train, or a too train. Adverbs and nouns never have anything to do with each other.

But there is one thing to watch out for. Some words play two parts and act as both adjectives and adverbs. *Fast* is one: *He caught the fast train . . . He ran fast.* There are many more: *We arrived in the early hours of the morning . . . We arrived early. It's hard work . . . He works hard.* If we want to know which part one of these dual-role words is playing we have to ask ourselves: what sort of word is it modifying?

Suddenly, when we had gone ten yards, the procession stopped short.

Is *short,* in that sentence, an adjective or an adverb? Does it tell us something about the procession, or something about the way it stopped?

The gallows stood in a small yard, separate from the main grounds of the prison, and overgrown with tall prickly weeds. It was a brick erection like three sides of a shed, with planking on top, and above that two beams and a crossbar with the rope dangling. The hangman, a grey-haired convict in the white uniform of the prison, was waiting beside his machine. He greeted us with a servile crouch as we entered. At a word from Francis the two warders, gripping the prisoner more closely than ever, half led, half pushed him to the gallows and helped him clumsily up the ladder. Then the hangman climbed up and fixed the rope round the prisoner's neck.

---

1 What kind of word is *more* in line 9? Make up a sentence in which it is used as a different kind of word.

2 Now turn back to page 8 and look at the second sentence of the extract. What kind of word is *still?* Make up a sentence in which it is used as a different kind of word.

3 *Uniform* (line 6) is a concrete noun. Make up a sentence to show that it can also be an adjective.

4 Now turn it into an adverb, by adding a suffix. Then by adding a different suffix turn it into an abstract noun.

5 *He greeted us with a servile crouch* . . . If you had to replace the phrase *with a servile crouch* with just one adverb, what one could you find that would convey *some* portion of the meaning? Write out the whole sentence, which will consist of four words.

6 Now look at the last sentence but one of the extract. Orwell doesn't tell us, directly, what the feelings of the two warders were towards the prisoner as they got him up the ladder. But *helped* and *clumsily* contain clues. What do these two words tell us, indirectly, about the warders' feelings?

7 *The two warders helped the prisoner clumsily up the ladder.* Write that sentence out again with another verb instead of *helped* and another adverb instead of *clumsily.* Choose words which will suggest, *indirectly,* that the warders had different feelings towards the prisoner from those suggested by *helped* and *clumsily.* Then briefly explain what those different feelings were.

8 Notice how grimly bare and factual the last sentence of Orwell's paragraph is. There are no adjectives and no adverbs of manner. Without using any yourself (except *dead* if you want it) describe what happened to the prisoner when the hangman pulled the lever. Do it in two or three sentences. Imagine that you are continuing Orwell's account and that he has already written: *The hangman pulled the lever.*

6 Prepositions

Prepositions are words like *at, in, of, by, with, from, between, above, against, under.* They do one job only: they introduce nouns.

The hangman fixed the rope round the prisoner's neck.

Round is a preposition, and it introduces the noun *neck.*

The hangman, a grey-haired convict in the white uniform of the prison, was waiting beside his machine.

In introduces *uniform; of* introduces *prison;* and *beside* introduces *machine.*

Now here is a sentence with the prepositions left out. It comes from the extract on page 10. Will you fill them in, and then turn back and see if you have put in what Orwell wrote:

The gallows stood —— a small yard, separate —— the main grounds —— the prison, and overgrown —— tall prickly weeds.

We stood waiting, five yards away. The warders had formed in a rough circle round the gallows. And then, when the noose was fixed, the prisoner began crying out to his god. It was a high, reiterated cry of 'Ram! Ram! Ram! Ram!' not urgent and fearful, but steady, rhythmical. The dog answered the sound with a whine. The hangman, still standing on the gallows, produced a small cotton bag and drew it down over the prisoner's face. But the sound, muffled by the cloth, still persisted: 'Ram! Ram! Ram! Ram! Ram!'

---

1   Will you now write down all the prepositions in that passage.
    There are eight, and each one occurs only once.

2   Orwell uses three adjectives – as well as *reiterated* – to tell us what
    the prisoner's cry was like. Which are they?

3   He adds two more to tell us what it was *not* like. Which are they?
    And why do you think he added them?

4   What kind of noun is *Ram*?

5   What kind of word is *still* in line 6?

6   Turn *circle* (line 2) and *face* (line 8) into adjectives by adapting their
    endings and adding suffixes.

7   Turn *urgent* (line 5) and *rhythmical* (line 5) into nouns. What kind
    of nouns are they?

8   The prisoner's cries and the dog's whine – how many contrasts
    between those two sounds can you think of? Set them out in a
    series of contrasting sentences. Here is one to start you off: 'One
    was steady; the other wavered'. When you have finished,
    underline all the adjectives you used.

9   The cotton bag muffled the prisoner's cries. In two or three
    sentences describe how some other sound was muffled by
    something else (the sound of traffic, perhaps, muffled by the
    shutting of a window . . . the sound of bells, or the shouts of a
    football crowd, muffled by a crossing breeze . . .).

0   In an earlier extract Orwell wrote: *The hangman greeted us with a
    —— crouch.* If you remember the adjective he used, write it down.
    If not, write down one that you think would be effective, and
    then turn to page 10 to see what he put.

1   Find a passage in a book or a newspaper containing five or six
    prepositions. Copy it out leaving blanks for them, and then hand
    it to your neighbour for him to fill them in.

7 Words that can be used as both prepositions and adverbs

A good many words can be: *in, on, before, behind, round, near, below, along, through, off* . . . and several more.

There is an easy way of telling which part they are playing. If the word is a preposition it always introduces a noun: *The warders gathered round the prisoner.* If it is an adverb it never does: *The warders gathered round. We marched along the road* . . . *We marched along quickly. There was a bowl of rice on the table* . . . *The procession moved on once more. The magistrates walked behind the warders* . . . *The magistrates walked behind.*

Will you now make up two sentences – one in which *before* is a preposition, and one in which it is an adverb.

The hangman climbed down and stood holding the lever. The steady, muffled crying from the prisoner, 'Ram! Ram! Ram!', never faltered for an instant. The superintendent, his head on his chest, was slowly poking the ground with his stick; perhaps the superintendent was counting the cries, allowing the prisoner a fixed number. Everyone had changed colour. The Indians had gone grey. We looked at the lashed, hooded man and listened to his cries – each cry another second of life; the same thought was in all our minds: oh, kill him quickly, stop that abominable noise!

---

1   There are four adverbs in that passage. Which are they?

2   One of those four words, if it were used in a different way, could be a preposition. Make up a sentence in which it is one.

3   Write down the eight prepositions that come in the passage. Each one occurs only once.

4   Three of those eight words, in different sentences, could be adverbs. Make up three sentences (one for each) in which they are. You may need to use a dictionary.

5   The superintendent was *slowly poking the ground with his stick.* In one sentence describe him performing some other slight action with his stick, and try to introduce an adverb as telling as *slowly.*

6   What suffix do we add to *colour* if we want to turn it into an adjective meaning *without colour?* Write down just the suffix, putting a hyphen in front of it . . .

7   . . . And what four nouns in the last two lines of the extract can have the same suffix added to them? Write them down with the suffix added.

8   Fill in the missing prepositions in this sentence: *The superintendent —— the jail, who was standing apart —— the rest —— us, moodily prodding the gravel —— his stick, raised his head —— the sound.* Then turn to page 4 to see if your prepositions are the same as Orwell's.

9   Who do you think felt the most sympathy for the prisoner – the superintendent, Francis, the hangman, or one of the Indian warders? Give reasons for your choice. (It might help to look back at some of the earlier extracts.)

10 And who do you think felt the least sympathy? Again give reasons.

8 Pronouns

Pronouns are words like *I, you, he, it, us, they, them*. Their job is to stand in place of a noun that has just been mentioned, so that the writer doesn't have to repeat it. They can also take the form of adjectives, like *my, his, your, their, its,* and so on.

These humble little words are extremely useful, for they make sentences flow lightly and easily. We would find it impossible to write fluent English if we didn't have them there, always on hand, ready to lighten our language at every turn, with their touches of neatness and economy. If a writer fails to use one when he has a chance of doing so, even just once, his English will immediately begin to sound heavy.

In the passage quoted on page 14 I altered one word: where Orwell put a pronoun I repeated the noun. Will you now read this passage again and see where my noun comes, and notice how it jars.

Suddenly the superintendent made up his mind. Throwing up his head he made a swift motion with his stick. 'Chalo!' he shouted almost fiercely.

There was a clanking noise, and then dead silence. The prisoner had vanished, and the rope was twisting on itself. I let go of the dog, and it galloped immediately to the back of the gallows; but when it got there it stopped short, barked, and then retreated into a corner of the yard, where it stood among the weeds, looking timorously out at us. We went round the gallows to inspect the prisoner's body. He was dangling with his toes pointed straight downwards, very slowly revolving, as dead as a stone.

The superintendent reached out with his stick and poked the bare brown body; it oscillated slightly. 'He's all right,' the superintendent said. He backed out from under the gallows, and blew out a deep breath.

1　Rewrite the following passage exactly as it stands but using the words *warder* and *prisoner* and *wrists* only once, and on every other occasion using pronouns instead: *The warder went up to the prisoner. The warder took hold of the prisoner's wrists and handcuffed his wrists so tightly that the prisoner was unable to move his arms. Then the warder ordered the prisoner to go back to his cell.* . . . Then read through what you have written and see if you think the meaning is clear.

2　The superintendent shouted 'Chalo!' *almost fiercely*. What does *almost fiercely* tell us about his feelings?

3　What kind of word is *short,* in line 7? Make up a sentence in which it is a different kind of word.

4　What kind of word is *timorously* (line 9)? Write down a word that means the opposite.

5　What kind of word is *round,* in line 10?

6　Quote the one adjective Orwell uses in the second paragraph of the passage. He uses it twice.

7　On one of the occasions on which he uses it it *could* have a double meaning. Explain how. Do you think he intended it to, or is this mere coincidence?

8　In a sentence consisting of only three words explain why the superintendent *blew out a deep breath*.

9　The onlookers, listening to the prisoner's cries, thought: *Oh, kill him quickly, stop that —— noise!* Choose an adjective to go there – the best one you can think of – and then look at the last sentence of the extract on page 14.

10　'*He's all right*.' The superintendent's remark could be said to be unintentionally ironic. Why?

9   Another pronoun: 'one'

One is a pronoun if it stands in place of a noun: *There were five cells in the yard. The one in the far corner was empty.*

If it modifies a noun it's an adjective: *One cell was empty.*

One is a useful word. Read this sentence, for example: *There were several puddles on the path, and after we'd gone a few yards I saw the prisoner step aside to avoid a puddle.* Now read it again, putting *one* in instead of the repeated noun, and see how much better it sounds.

None is short for *not one.* Nothing could be more singular than *one,* and so if we want to stick to the rules we have to write: *None of the prisoners was ready.* But language is formed by life, not rules, and there are many writers who would put: *None of the prisoners were ready.* Which do you prefer?

The warders unfixed bayonets and marched away. We walked into the big central yard of the prison. The convicts, under the command of warders armed with lathis, were already receiving their breakfast. The convicts squatted in long rows, each man holding a tin pannikin, while two warders with buckets marched round ladling out rice; it seemed quite a homely, jolly scene, after the hanging. An enormous relief had come upon us now that the job was done. One felt an impulse to sing, to break into a run, to snigger. All at once everyone began chattering gaily.

•

1 I took out one of Orwell's pronouns and put in its place the noun it stood for. What pronoun did I take out, and what line did I take it out of?

2 What pronoun could Orwell have used instead of *one* in the last sentence but one?

3 What kind of word is *away,* in the first sentence?

4 Sometimes, in an expression to do with sport, *away* is twisted round to serve as an adjective. Make up a sentence in which it is used in this way.

5 What kind of word is *round,* in line 6?

6 Make up a sentence in which it's a preposition . . .

7 . . . an adjective

8 . . . a noun.

9 The meal seemed *quite a homely, jolly scene, after the hanging.* Write down two adjectives which would show that the hanging was quite the opposite of *homely* or *jolly.*

10 By adding suffixes turn *homely* and *jolly* into nouns. What kind of nouns are they?

11 Turn the two adjectives you found for question 9 into nouns.

12 What noun means much the same as *impulse* (line 9) and could be put there instead of it without altering the meaning?

13 Turn *impulse* into an adjective by adding a suffix.

14 Try to imagine what the *big central yard of the prison* was like, and describe it in a few sentences. You could, if you wanted to, introduce details about sounds, and even about smells, as well as visual ones.

10 More pronouns: 'this' and 'that'

This and *that* often serve as pronouns in a special way of
their own. Instead of standing in place of a noun they refer
back to some fact or some circumstance that has just been
mentioned:

*The condemned men had no idea when the executions were going
to take place. This increased the tension terribly.*

This refers back to the fact that the men didn't know when
they were going to be executed.

This and *that* should only be used to refer back to a
remark in this way when a single clear idea has emerged
uppermost from it.

*The cells were overcrowded, and the food was so bad that during
the previous week one prisoner had died. This was a cause of great
worry for the prison governor.*

In that piece of writing no single idea has emerged; so the
this has nothing to cling to, and it floats meaninglessly.

This and *that* are pronouns only if they stand on their
own. If they modify nouns (*this week, that house*) they are
adjectives.

Francis was walking by the superintendent, talking
garrulously: 'Well, sir, all hass passed off with the utmost
satisfactoriness. It was all finished – flick! like that. It iss not
always so – oah, no! I have known cases where the doctor
wass obliged to go beneath the gallows and pull the
prisoner's legs to ensure decease. Most disagreeable!'

'Wriggling about, eh? That's bad,' said the
superintendent.

'Ach, sir, it iss worse when they become refractory!
One man, I recall, clung to the bars of hiss cage when we
went to take him out. It took six warders to dislodge him.
"My dear fellow," we said, "think of all the pain and
trouble you are causing to us!" '

I found that I was laughing quite loudly. Everyone was
laughing. Even the superintendent grinned. 'You'd better all

come out and have a drink,' he said quite genially. 'I've got a bottle of whisky in the car.'

We went through the big double gates into the road. We all had a drink together, native and European alike, quite amicably. The dead man was a hundred yards away.

---

1   What kind of word is *that*, in the second paragraph of the extract?

2   What kind of word is *that* in the last sentence of the extract on page 14?

3   Turn *genially* (line 16) into a noun.

4   Write down a word that means the opposite of *genially*, and then turn that word into a noun too.

5   What kind of word is *amicably* (in the last line)? By altering its ending turn it into an adjective. What other adjective has much the same meaning?

6   Francis was *talking garrulously*. How does a person talk who talks garrulously? Why do you think Francis started talking in that way?

7   Francis evidently knew a bit of grammar, since he formed an abstract noun from an adjective in the correct way. But the noun he formed is hardly ever used and sounds slightly comic. Which noun is it?

8   What kind of word is *refractory* (line 9)? Explain its meaning – guessing it from the context if you don't know it. Then compare your definition of it with what a dictionary says.

9   Why do you think Francis used such an unusual word?

10   In another place he put in a preposition where he shouldn't have done. Where?

11   We have come to know the superintendent as a moody, irritable man. What word in the extract reminds us that he was that sort of person?

12   Why does it remind us of this?

Verbs

Extracts taken from

Cecil Woodham-Smith's account of
The Charge of The Light Brigade

11 Finite verbs

Verbs appear in different forms. Usually they appear in one or other of their tenses. It may be a past tense (*the superintendent raised his hand*), or a present tense (*the superintendent is raising his hand*), or a future tense (*the superintendent will raise his hand*). Or it may be some other more complicated tense. Verbs are being truest to their nature when they appear in this form, for then they are doing the job that only they can do – making something happen at a given time.

When a verb appears in this way – wearing, as it were, the dress of one of its tenses – it is said to be a verb in its finite form. This is a clumsy expression, so for convenience we say instead that it is a finite verb. *Raised* is a finite verb. So is *is raising*. So is *will raise*.★

We will look now at some extracts from a description of the charge of the Light Brigade. They are taken from The Reason Why, *by Cecil Woodham-Smith. This famous charge took place in 1854, during the Crimean War, as a result of a misleading and ambiguous order which required the Brigade to advance down a valley straight towards the Russian guns. The order was delivered by a Captain Nolan.*

The Brigade advanced with beautiful precision. Lord Cardigan rode alone at their head, a brilliant and gallant figure. He wore the gorgeous uniform of the 11th Hussars. The bright sunlight lit up the brilliance of cherry colour and royal blue, the richness of fur and plume and lace. He rode his favourite charger, Ronald, 'a thoroughbred chestnut of great beauty', and as he led his Brigade steadily down the valley towards the guns, he seemed, as his aide-de-camp Sir George Wombwell wrote, 'the very incarnation of bravery'.

★ *Finite* is a word borrowed from Latin grammar. In English grammar it's little more than a label. But it's a very useful one.

1   There are eight finite verbs in that extract. Write them down. They are all in the same tense. What tense is it – past, present or future?

2   What kind of noun is *precision* (line 1)? What adjective corresponds to it?

3   What adjective corresponds to *incarnation* (in the last sentence)? It has one syllable fewer than the noun. Make up a sentence in which it is used. Look in a dictionary if you need to.

4   Another adjective, of only two syllables, can be formed from the central part of *incarnation*. What adjective is this, and what does it mean? Again, use a dictionary.

5   . . . *a brilliant and gallant figure*. Turn *brilliant* and *gallant* into nouns. What kind of nouns are they?

6   There are only two adverbs in the extract – one in the second sentence, the other in the last. Which are they, and what words do they modify?

7   *Very* is nearly always used as an adverb, modifying either an adjective or another adverb. Give an example of it modifying first an adjective (two words), and then another adverb (two words again).

8   What kind of word does *very* modify in the last sentence of the extract? And what kind of word is it there?

9   The author creates a colourful picture. Which adjectives contribute to this effect?

10   Which nouns contribute to it too?

11   In a short paragraph write a description of a scene of pageantry (a military parade, perhaps, or a colourful wedding). Make it glow as splendidly as you can. But don't overdo it. Restraint is nearly always more effective than excess.

12 Verbal adjectives, or participles, that end in '-ing'

Verbs can also appear in forms *other* than those of their tenses – in forms which are *not* finite, and which do *not* make something happen at a given time.

Then, raising his right hand, he took the oath.

The expression *raising his right hand* doesn't make that man raise his hand at any particular time: the time is fixed by the finite verb *took*. We could switch it into the future, for example, and *raising* wouldn't alter:

Then, raising his right hand, he will take the oath.

Raising his right hand gives us a picture of the man *as* he took the oath. It describes him. It is doing the work of an adjective. *Raising* in that sentence is called a verbal adjective – or, more strictly, a participle.

But as well as behaving in that way, like adjectives, participles can also form *part* of a finite verb. *He was raising his hand. That* makes him do it at a given time. So does, for example, *is raising,* or *will be raising.* Those are finite verbs because the little words that come in front of *raising* lock it, as it were, into a tense.

Before the Light Brigade had advanced fifty yards the Russian guns crashed out, and great clouds of smoke rose at the end of the valley. A moment later an extraordinary and inexplicable incident took place. The advance was proceeding at a steady trot when suddenly Nolan, riding beside his friend Captain Morris in the first line, urged on his horse and galloped diagonally across the front. Galloping madly ahead and to the right, he crossed in front of Lord Cardigan – an unprecedented breach of military etiquette – and, turning in his saddle, shouted and waved his sword as if he would address the Brigade. Had he suddenly realized that his interpretation of the order had been wrong, and that in his impetuosity he had directed the Light Brigade to certain death? No one will ever know, because at that moment . . .

---

1 In that extract there is one finite verb that consists of two words, and the second of the two is a participle ending in *ing*. Write down this verb.

2 Now write down all the verbal adjectives – that is, all the participles with *-ing* endings which do *not* form part of a finite verb; and after each one write down the noun it modifies – that is to say, the noun that is performing the action it names.

3 By changing its suffix turn *suddenly* (line 5) into a noun.

4 What kind of noun is *interpretation* (line 12)? What verb is it derived from?

5 What suffix do we have to add to that verb in order to turn it into a noun meaning *a person who interprets?* Write down just the suffix, putting a hyphen in front of it.

6 In what other way is this suffix sometimes spelt? Can you think of a noun which ends with it spelt in this other way?

7 What adjective corresponds to *impetuosity* (line 13)? Can you think of another adjective that has much the same meaning? And of one that means the opposite?

8 Many words serve as both nouns and verbs; often only the context shows us which kind of word they are. In the third sentence there are three words which are nouns and which in different contexts could be verbs. Which words are these? Make up three sentences (one for each) in which they are verbs.

9 Complete this sentence by using the appropriate part of the verb *to wave:* Then —— *his sword, Nolan galloped across the front of the advancing Brigade.*

10 What part of the verb *to wave* is the word you used? What noun does it describe, or modify? (In other words, what noun is doing the waving?). And in the completed sentence which is the finite verb?

13   Verbal adjectives, or participles, that end in '-ed'*

Then the prisoner, escorted by the two warders, went back to his cell.

Escorted, in that sentence, is not related to any particular time, and so it is not a finite verb. The time is fixed by *went.* We could make the prisoner go back at a quite different time – we could say *will go back,* for example, instead of *went back* – and *escorted* won't change. Try, and you will see.

Escorted is another kind of verbal adjective, or participle. It describes the circumstances of the prisoner as he went back. He might have been a tall prisoner, or a thin one; as it happens, he was an escorted one.

But again, a participle of this kind can be *part* of a finite verb. If we put a word like *have* or *had* in front of *escorted* we make it part of one, because then we lock it into a tense and make something happen in a framework of time. *The warders have escorted the prisoner back to his cell. Have escorted* is a finite verb. And *escorted* on its own is a finite verb in a sentence like this one – *The warders escorted the prisoner back to his cell* – because there it's a different kind of word entirely, and not a participle at all: it's the past tense of the verb.

. . . No one will ever know, because at that moment a Russian shell burst on the right of Lord Cardigan, and a fragment tore its way into Nolan's breast, exposing his heart. The sword fell from Nolan's hand, but his right arm was still erect, and his body remained rigid in the saddle. His horse wheeled and began to gallop back through the advancing Brigade, and then from the body there burst a strange and appalling cry, a shriek so unearthly as to freeze the blood of all who heard him. The terrified horse carried the body, still shrieking, through the 4th Light Dragoons, and then at last Nolan fell from the saddle, dead.

---

* Or in an equivalent ending if the verb is irregular. For example, *protect* turns into *protected;* but *break* turns into *broken, lose* into *lost, bend* into *bent,* and so on.

4 Four words in the extract end in *-ed*. Three are finite verbs and one is a verbal adjective, or participle. Say which is which.

2 There are also four participles that end in *-ing*. Two of them come immediately in front of the nouns they modify, like ordinary adjectives. Write these down first, together with the nouns that follow them. Then write down the other two, and after each one write down the noun it modifies – that is to say, the noun that is doing what the participle says it is doing.

3 In the first sentence there is a word which is a verb but which in a different context could be a noun. Make up a sentence in which it is a noun.

6 *Exposing* (line 3) is part of the verb *to expose*. What is the corresponding noun?

7 I took out one of the author's pronouns and put in its place the noun it stood for. Which pronoun did I take out, and what line did I take it out of?

8 By adding a prefix turn *body* (line 5) into a verb. Then by adding a second prefix turn the meaning of this verb into the opposite.

9 By adding a suffix of two syllables turn *rigid* (line 5) into a noun. What kind of noun is it?

10 The last sentence of the extract ends forcefully. How did the author achieve this effect?

1 The writer creates a horrifying picture of Nolan's death. The horror derives to some extent from the way in which a particular noun is used. Which noun? And why does it have a horrifying effect?

2 In a short paragraph describe a person being killed in some way other than in battle. Make it horrifying. But remember that control and restraint usually make for vivid writing, and that overdoing it nearly always spoils the effect.

14 Wrongly related participles

Verbal adjectives, or participles, usually go with nouns, in order to describe them or modify them, just as ordinary adjectives do.

Then, raising his right hand, the judge pronounced sentence.

Raising goes with *judge:* it describes him as doing something.

It's a good idea to make sure verbal adjectives go with the *right* noun.

Riding home later that evening, a strange sight came into view.

That one doesn't. A writer who is careless over such matters can make some quite ridiculous things happen.

Lord Cardigan, looking strictly straight ahead and not aware of Nolan's death, was transported with fury. It was his impression that Nolan had been trying to take the command of the Brigade away from him; and so intense was his rage that when he was asked what he thought about as he advanced towards the guns, he replied that his mind was entirely occupied with anger against Nolan.

The first few hundred yards of the advance of the Light Brigade covered the same ground, whether the attack was to be on the guns on the Causeway Heights or the guns at the end of the valley. The Russians assumed that the redoubts were to be charged, but the Light Brigade, incredibly, made no attempt to wheel. With a gasp of horror, the watchers saw the lines of horsemen continue straight on down the North Valley.

The Russian artillery and riflemen on the Fedioukine Hills and the slopes of the Causeway Heights were absolutely taken by surprise. It was not possible to believe that this small force trotting down the North Valley in such beautiful order intended to attempt an attack on the battery at the end of the valley, intended to expose itself to a cross-fire of the most frightful and deadly kind, to which it had no possibility of replying. There was a moment's pause, and then from the Fedioukine Hills on one side and the

Causeway Heights on the other, battalion upon battalion of riflemen, battery upon battery of guns, poured down fire on the Light Brigade.

---

1   In the first sentence what noun do *looking* and *aware* modify? What kind of noun is it?

2   From the first paragraph pick out a finite verb that consists of three words.

3   In one place in the first paragraph there are three adverbs in a row. Which words are these?

4   We learn what Lord Cardigan's thoughts were as he advanced towards the guns. What do they reveal of his character?

5   *So intense was his rage . . . Intense* is a better adjective than *great* would have been. Why?

6   What prefix is often put in front of *occupied* (line 7) to reinforce the meaning it has in this sentence?

7   What kind of word is *straight* in the last sentence of the middle paragraph? What other kind of word could it be in a different context? Make up a sentence in which it is this other kind of word. What suffix do we add to it to turn it into a verb?

8   *It was not possible to believe . . .* What adverb in the second paragraph do these words echo?

9   *The Russian guns —— out.* Complete the sentence by putting in a finite verb. Then see what the author wrote (page 26).

10   Imagine that you were one of the Russian gunners who were watching from the heights as the Brigade began its advance down the North Valley. Describe two conflicting emotions you might have felt during the moment's pause before you opened fire.

11   Make up a sentence with a wrongly related participle in it and hand it to your neighbour for him to correct.

15   Verbal nouns, or gerunds

By adding *-ing* onto the end of itself a verb can make itself like a noun.

He loved fighting.

Fighting in that sentence is like a noun. We could put one in its place: *He loved a fight.*

He was accused of behaving like a coward.

We could put a noun instead of *behaving: He was accused of cowardly behaviour.*

Maintaining discipline was not easy.

We could have said: *The maintenance of discipline was not easy.*

    A verb that has added *-ing* to itself so that it can behave like a noun is called a verbal noun, or a gerund. Gerunds always *look* exactly the same as participles that end in *-ing;* but there is a big difference between them – the difference between a noun and an adjective.★

When advancing cavalry are caught in a withering fire and are too courageous to think of retreat, it is their instinct to quicken their pace, to gallop forward as fast as individual horses will carry them and get to grips with the enemy as soon as possible. But Lord Cardigan tightly restrained the pace of the Light Brigade: the line was to advance with parade-ground perfection. The inner squadron of the 17th Lancers broke into a canter. Captain White, its leader, was, he said, 'frankly anxious to get out of such a murderous fire and into the guns as being the lesser of two evils', and he shot forward, level with his brigadier. Lord Cardigan checked Captain White instantly. Lowering his sword and laying it across Captain White's breast, he told him sharply not to ride level with his commanding officer and not to force the pace.

★ *Gerund* is another name borrowed from Latin grammar. There is no point in going into its meaning because when it's applied to English grammar it hasn't got any. It's better to recognize it for what it is – an ugly label.

1 Five words in the extract end in *-ing,* and they are all verbal adjectives (or participles). Write them down and after each one write the noun it modifies – that is to say, the noun that is carrying out the action named by the participle.

2 Now choose any one of those five words which you wrote down as being participles, and make up a sentence in which it is used as a verbal noun (or gerund).

3 There is a verbal noun (or gerund) in the last paragraph of the extract on page 30. Which word is this?

4 What kind of noun is *instinct* (line 2)? Form an adjective from it by adding a suffix.

5 What kind of word is *forward* in the first sentence? Make up a sentence in which it is a different kind of word.

6 What aspect of Lord Cardigan's character is suggested by the adverb *tightly* (line 5)?

7 What kind of word is *parade-ground,* in line 7? If you find it difficult to decide, look back to question 4 on page 5.

8 Why do you think Lord Cardigan wanted to restrain the pace of the Brigade and make it advance with *parade-ground perfection?*

9 What kind of noun is *perfection?* By adding a prefix to it turn it into a noun that means the opposite. Then, by adding a suffix to it, turn it into a noun that means *a person who believes in perfection.*

10 Captain White's actual words are quoted. Why do you think he prefaced his remark with the adverb *frankly?*

11 I have replaced one of the author's pronouns with the noun it stands for. Find the sentence in which I did that, and then write it out again with the pronoun put back.

16   The infinitive

The infinitive is the verb's name. A *to* often comes into it. *To wander, to sigh, to sleep* – that's how we name those verbs. But there isn't always a *to* in front. It's never there in a dictionary, for example; but when you look up *wander* it's the infinitive you are looking at. In some sentences the *to* is there:

He ordered them to leave . . . He wanted me to go . . . They promised to come . . . The earth began to shake.

In others it isn't:

He made them leave . . . I shall go . . . They could come tomorrow . . . They felt the earth shake.

The infinitive is one of those parts of the verb that are not finite. Its name tells us that.

All Lord Cardigan could see at the end of the valley was a white bank of smoke, through which from time to time flashed great tongues of flame marking the position of the guns. He chose one which seemed to be about the centre of the battery and rode steadily for it, neither turning in his saddle nor moving his head. Erect, rigid and dauntless, his bearing contributed enormously to the steadiness, the astonishing discipline which earned the Charge of the Light Brigade immortality.

The fire grew fiercer. The first line was now within range of the guns at the end of the valley, as well as the fire pouring from both flanks. Round-shot, grape and shells began to mow men down not singly, but by groups. The pace quickened and quickened again, and the trot became a canter.

---

1. There are three infinitives in the extract – two with a *to* in front and one without one. Which are they?

2. Now turn back to the extract on page 30 and look at the middle paragraph. Can you find there an infinitive that does not have a *to* in front of it?

3. *Marking, turning,* and *moving,* in the first paragraph, are participles. Make up three sentences, one for each, in which they are gerunds.

4. *To mark, to turn, to move:* make up three sentences in which those verbs are used in their finite form.

5. *Erect, rigid, dauntless* . . . Choose three other adjectives which would create a similar picture of Lord Cardigan.

6. Why do you think Lord Cardigan's bearing contributed to the steadiness of the Brigade? Answer in one sentence.

7. Which are the finite verbs in the second and third sentences?

8. Turn *discipline* (line 8) into a word meaning a *person who believes in strict discipline.*

9. Now make up a sentence in which *discipline* is used as a verb.

10. What adjective corresponds to *immortality* (line 9)?

11. Will you now complete this sentence: *Tennyson's poem is dedicated to the men of the Light Brigade, and it —— their heroism.* The missing word is the verb that corresponds to the adjective you wrote down for question 10.

12. *A fragment of shell —— its way into Nolan's breast.* What verb would come in well there? Choose the most effective one you can think of, and then turn back to page 28 to see what the author put.

17 A summary of the parts of the verb that are not finite

There are three parts of the verb that are not finite: the participle (two kinds), the gerund, and the infinitive.

Participles are verbal adjectives. Some end in *-ing* (*then, raising his right hand, the judge pronounced sentence*), and some end in *-ed,* or in an equivalent irregular ending (*the prisoner, escorted by the two warders, made his way back to his cell*).

Gerunds, which look exactly like the participles that end in *-ing,* are verbal nouns (*he loved fighting*).

The infinitive is the verb's name. Sometimes it has a *to* (*he ordered them to leave*), and sometimes it doesn't (*he made them leave*).

Eight minutes had now passed since the advance began, and Lord Cardigan, with the survivors of the first line hard on his heels, galloping furiously but steadily, was within a few yards of the battery. The troopers could see the faces of the gunners, and Lord Cardigan selected the particular space between two guns where he intended to enter. At that moment there was a roar, the earth trembled, huge flashes of flame shot out and the smoke became so dense that darkness seemed to fall. The Russian gunners had fired a salvo from their twelve guns into the first line of the Light Brigade at a distance of eighty yards. Lord Cardigan's charger Ronald was blown sideways by the blast, a torrent of flame seemed to belch down his right side, and for a moment he thought he had lost a leg. Lord Cardigan was, he estimated, only two or three lengths from the mouths of the guns. Then, wrenching Ronald's head round, he drove into the smoke and, charging into the space he had previously selected, was the first man into the battery.

. . . *galloping furiously but steadily*. What noun does this expression describe, or modify? (In other words, who was doing the galloping?) If you think that the author hasn't made this clear enough, say so, and explain why.

In the extract there are two more participles that end in -*ing*. Write them down, and after each one write down the noun they modify (in other words, the noun that is carrying out the action they name).

What verb corresponds to *survivors* (line 2)? And what noun?

What kind of word is *hard* in the first sentence? Make up a sentence in which it is a different kind of word.

What part of the verb is *see* in the second sentence?

Turn *particular* (line 5) into a verb, putting a *to* in front.

What noun corresponds to *furiously* (line 3)? And to *intended* (line 6)? And to *enter* (line 6)?

The men of the Light Brigade were *caught in a —— fire.* For the adjective there the author used a participle ending in -*ing*. Write down one that would sound well, and then turn back to the first sentence of the extract on page 32 and compare it with the one the author chose.

Round shot, grape and shells began to —— men down. What verb would be effective there? Choose one, and then see what the author put by turning to the last paragraph on page 34. What part of the verb is it?

The troopers could see the faces of the gunners. Imagine that you were one of those troopers, and that you caught a glimpse – fleeting but clear – of just one Russian gunner. Describe, in close detail, what you saw.

18　Auxiliary verbs

Lord Cardigan waves his sword. Waves is a verb in the present tense. By making a small alteration to the ending of it we can turn the present into the past: *Lord Cardigan waved his sword.*

Those two tenses – the simple present and the simple past – are the only two we can form in that economical way, by using just one word which we change slightly. To form any of the others we have to enlist the help of little tense-forming verbs called auxiliary verbs. There are six of them: *to be* (*am, is, was,* and so on); *to have; do, does* and *did; shall* and *should; will* and *would;* and *may* and *might.* These little verbs, combined in various ways, form all the other tenses in our language: *Lord Cardigan is waving his sword . . . he will wave it . . . he will be waving it . . . he did wave it . . . he had been waving it . . . he may have been waving it . . . he would have waved it . . .* and so on.

When Lord Cardigan dashed into the battery he had, by a miracle, passed through the gap between the two guns unhurt, and in a few seconds was clear. He neither turned back nor paused. His charger was wild with excitement, and before he could be checked Lord Cardigan had been carried to within twenty yards of the Russians. For a moment they stared at each other, the Russians utterly astonished by the sudden apparition of this solitary horseman, gorgeous and glittering with gold. By an amazing coincidence, one of the officers, Prince Radzivill, recognized Lord Cardigan – they had met in London at dinners and balls – and the Prince detached a troop of Cossacks with instructions to capture him alive. The Cossacks approached him, but did not attempt to cut him down, and after a short encounter in which he received a slight wound on the thigh he evaded them by wheeling his horse, galloped back through the guns again, and came out almost where, only a few minutes earlier, he had dashed in.

---

1 What adverb could stand in place of *by a miracle* in the first sentence?

2 What kind of word is *unhurt,* in the first sentence? And what noun does it modify?

3 *Wild with excitement* (line 4) . . . *glittering with gold* (line 9). Those two expressions are not quite identical in their grammatical structure. What is the difference between them?

4 In the extract there is one participle, ending in *-ing,* which is used immediately in front of the noun it modifies, like an ordinary adjective. Which word is this?

5 What noun corresponds to *solitary* (line 8)? It has one syllable fewer.

6 What part of the verb is *wheeling* in the last sentence?

7 *A torrent of flame seemed to —— down his right side.* Choose a verb that would complete that sentence in a vivid way. Then compare your choice with the author's by looking back to the extract on page 36, line 13. What part of the verb is it?

8 What kind of word is the last word in the extract? Make up a sentence in which it is a different kind of word.

9 Find two words in the last sentence which are nouns but which in different contexts could be verbs, and make up two sentences (one for each) in which they are verbs.

10 The author could have written *appearance* in line 8, instead of *apparition.* But *apparition* adds a meaning that *appearance* would not have given. What shade of meaning does it add?

19 'To be', 'to have', and 'to do' as verbs in their own right

These three verbs, as well as playing an auxiliary, tense-forming part, can also stand independently, as verbs in their own right. *The smoke was very thick. He had a sword in his hand. He did a curious thing. Was, had,* and *did* in those sentences are all finite verbs.

Lord Cardigan, looking up the valley over the scene of the charge, could see no sign of his brigade. The valley was strewn with dead and dying; small groups of men wounded or unhorsed were struggling towards the British lines; both his aides-de-camp had vanished; he had ridden never once looking back, and he had no idea of what the fate of his brigade had been. Nor had he any feeling of responsibility. In his own words, having 'led the Brigade and launched them with due impetus, he considered his duty was done'. The idea of trying to find out what had happened to his men or of rallying the survivors never crossed his mind. With extraordinary indifference to danger he had led the Light Brigade down the valley as if he were leading a charge in a review in Hyde Park, and he now continued to behave as if he were in a review in Hyde Park. He had, however, some apprehension that for a general his isolated position was unusual, and he avoided any undignified appearance of haste by riding back very slowly, most of the time at a walk.

As he rode he continued to brood on Nolan's behaviour, and on nothing else; and when he reached the point where the Heavy Brigade was halted, he rode up to General Scarlett and immediately broke into accusations of Nolan, furiously complaining of Nolan's insubordination. Lord Cardigan finished contemptuously, 'Imagine the fellow screaming like a woman when he was hit'. General Scarlett checked him: 'Say no more, my lord; you have just ridden over Captain Nolan's dead body.'

---

1. In the first paragraph the word *had* appears eight times. Sometimes it is an auxiliary verb, and sometimes it stands independently. Look through the paragraph, and every time you come to a *had* write either 'aux.' or 'ind.'

2. Now do the same for the three *were*s in the first paragraph.

3. What adjective corresponds to *apprehension* (in the last sentence of the first paragraph)?

4. What kind of word is *riding* (in the same sentence)? And what kind of word introduces it?

5. Can you find two more words in this paragraph of the same kind as *riding*?

6. The idea of finding out what had happened to his men never crossed Lord Cardigan's mind. What sort of man does this attitude reveal? Answer briefly, and try to introduce some carefully considered adjectives.

7. Complete this sentence by using the appropriate part of the verb *to wrench*: Then, —— Ronald's head round, Lord Cardigan drove into the smoke.

8. What part of the verb *to wrench* is the word you used? What noun does it modify? (In other words, what noun is doing the wrenching?) And in the completed sentence which is the finite verb?

9. Lord Cardigan was *contemptuous* when he spoke about Nolan. *Contemptuous* means *showing contempt*. By altering its ending change it into a word that means *deserving contempt*.

10. Lord Cardigan, you will remember, had received a slight wound on the thigh. Imagine that General Scarlett glanced down and noticed it. Describe what he saw.

Nouns and verbs

Extracts taken from

D. H. Lawrence:
The Rainbow

20 Subject, verb, object

There is space and there is time. Things exist in a certain state at a given moment, and these things act on each other as time passes. That is all there is in reality and all there is in language. There are nouns and there are verbs.

If a thing acts in such a way that what it does seems to be confined to itself, there will be a noun and a verb: *Flowers bloom.*

If it acts in such a way as to affect some other thing, there will be a noun, a verb, and another noun: *Storms destroy crops.*

The noun that carries through the action is said to be the subject of the verb. *Flowers* is the subject of *bloom*. *Storms* is the subject of *destroy*. The noun that is acted on is said to be the object of the verb. *Crops* is the object of *destroy*.

The extracts that follow come from The Rainbow, *by D. H. Lawrence.*

He began to go away from home. He went to Nottingham on Saturdays, always alone, to the football match and to the music-hall. With his hard, golden-brown eyes, so keen-seeing with their tiny black pupils, he watched all the people.

In the Empire one evening he sat next to two girls. He was aware of the girl beside him. She was rather small, common, with a fresh complexion and an upper lip that lifted from her teeth, so that, when she was not conscious, her mouth was slightly open and her lips pressed outwards in a kind of blind appeal. She was strongly aware of the man next to her, so that all her body was still, very still. Her face watched the stage. Her arms went down into her lap, very self-conscious and still.

A gleam lit up in him: should he begin with her? Should he begin with her to live the other, the unadmitted life of his desire? Why not? He had always been so good.

Save for his wife, he was a virgin. He wanted the other life. His own life was barren, not enough. He wanted the other.

---

1   Write down the three words in the third sentence that are the subject, the verb, and the object . . .

2   . . . and the three that are the subject, the verb, and the object in the last sentence but one of the second paragraph.

3   Find a sentence that has only a subject and a verb in it and no object, and write the two words down.

4   . . . *her lips pressed outwards in a kind of blind appeal* (line 10). The verb in that sentence is an unexpected choice. What does it contribute to the description?

5   What kind of word is *gleam,* in the first sentence of the last paragraph? What is the corresponding adjective? It is a special kind of adjective. What kind?

6   I took a pronoun out of the middle paragraph and put in its place the noun it stood for. What word did I take out?

7   By adding a suffix turn *barren* (in the last sentence but one) into a noun. What adjective means the opposite of *barren?* Turn that adjective into a noun too.

8   What kind of word is *one* (line 6)?

9   The man couldn't see the further girl so clearly; but we will suppose that he caught some glimpses of her. Explain what glimpses he caught, and describe what she looked like from his point of view.

10 Lawrence wrote (line 13) *Her face watched the stage* – not *She watched the stage.* There is a subtle difference. Can you explain what it is?

21 Transitive and intransitive verbs

A finite verb always has a subject, but it doesn't always have an object.

The stage-manager lowered the curtain.

If it does have one, as *lowered* has in that sentence, it is called a transitive verb. A transitive verb always has to push forward until it arrives at a noun which it can claim as its object. If we just said *The stage-manager lowered* the sense would not be complete because *lowered,* a transitive verb, would be left unfulfilled, with no noun to go to.

Suddenly the procession stopped.

The verb hasn't got an object in that sentence, and it doesn't need one. The action reaches its completion at exactly the same moment as we finish reading the word *stopped.* *Stopped,* in that sentence, is an intransitive verb.

But the verb *to stop* isn't always intransitive. Like many other verbs in the English language – most of them, in fact – it can be used both transitively and intransitively.

The police stopped the procession.

In that sentence it is transitive.

Her open mouth, showing the small, irregular, white teeth, appealed to him. It was open and ready. It was so vulnerable. Why should he not go in and enjoy what was there? The slim arm that went down so still and motionless to the lap, it was pretty. Her childishness whetted him keenly.

'That was the best turn we've had,' he said to her, leaning over as he clapped his hands.

The girl started, turned round, her eyes lit up with an almost painful flash of a smile, the colour came deeply in her cheeks.

'Yes, it was,' she said, quite meaninglessly, and she covered her rather prominent teeth with her lips. Then she sat looking straight before her, seeing nothing, only conscious of the colour burning in her cheeks.

All the verbs in the third paragraph of the extract are used intransitively. Three of them, in different contexts, could be used transitively. Make up three sentences (one for each) in which they are.

A participle ending in -*ing* can have an object. There are two in the extract that have. Quote them, and after each one quote the noun that stands as the object.

. . . *with an almost painful flash of a smile* . . . What does that smile tell us about the girl's feelings at that moment?

By adding a prefix turn *vulnerable* into a word meaning the opposite.

By adding a prefix change the meaning of *covered* into the opposite. *To cover:* what other prefixes can be added to this verb? Write the whole word down, each time.

. . . *her lips pressed outwards in a kind of —— appeal*. Do you remember the very effective adjective that Lawrence used there? If you do, write it down. If not, suggest one that you think would do well and then compare it with Lawrence's by turning back to the middle paragraph of the extract on page 44.

What word that is an adjective in the first sentence could be a verb in a different context? Make up a sentence in which it is a verb.

. . . *she covered her rather prominent teeth with her lips.* Which two adjectives in the extract – one in this sentence and one in an earlier sentence – suggest, indirectly, the unconscious motive behind this action?

In a short paragraph, that could be fitted in between the first and second paragraphs of the extract, describe the turn that was going on on the stage, and say how it ended.

Think of three verbs that can be used both transitively and intransitively, and make up three sentences in which they are used intransitively. Then hand what you have written to your neighbour. His task will be to make up three sentences in which those verbs are used transitively.

Verbs have an active form and a passive form. The active form is the one they take when we use them in a straightforward way:

The police stopped the procession.

It is the direct, natural form. When it is used the subject (*police*) drives straight through to the verb (*stopped*), and the verb – if it is transitive – drives straight through to the object (*procession*).

The passive form is more devious:

The procession was stopped by the police.

The natural order is reversed. The object (*procession*) is taken out of its place after the verb and made the subject of it; and at the same time the verb is altered by means of an auxiliary verb into the passive, so as to keep the general meaning of the sentence the same (*stopped* is altered to *was stopped*).

The passive form comes naturally into use when the *sufferer* of the action is the centre of interest. *The prisoner was brought out of his cell. He was handcuffed, and his arms were lashed to his sides.* Here our interest is focussed on the prisoner and on what he had done to him, not on who did it.

'It's not such a good programme as last week's,' he said.

Again she half turned her face to him, and her clear, bright eyes, bright like shallow water, filled with light, frightened, yet involuntarily lighting and shaking with response.

'Oh isn't it! I wasn't able to come last week.'

He noted the common accent. It pleased him. He knew what class she came of. Probably she was a warehouse-lass. He was glad she was a common girl.

He proceeded to tell her about the last week's programme. She answered at random, very confusedly. The colour burned in her cheek. Yet she always answered him. The girl on the other side sat remotely, obviously silent. He ignored her.

He saw the performance drawing to a close. His senses were alert and wilful. He would press his advantages. He followed her and her plain friend down the stairs to the street. It was raining.

---

1 *He ignored her.* Turn that sentence into the passive . . .

2 . . . and this one: *The critics did not praise last week's programme very highly.*

3 Is *filled,* in line 4, a finite verb or a participle?

4 What part of the verb is *frightened,* in the same sentence?

5 *Her open mouth was so ——.* The adjective Lawrence used means, literally, *easily wounded.* Write it down if you can remember it. It comes in the third line of the extract on page 46.

6 What adjective corresponds to *involuntarily* (line 5)? By leaving out the prefix turn it into an adjective that means the opposite, and then write down the verb that corresponds to that adjective.

7 What word does the adverb *remotely* modify (line 14)?

8 The other girl *sat remotely, obviously silent.* By means of just two adverbs and an adjective Lawrence gives us an insight into that girl's attitude, and even into her thoughts. What insight do those words give us?

9 Turn *probably* (line 9) into an adjective. What noun corresponds to this adjective? By adding a prefix change the meaning of the adjective into the opposite.

10 Before the final sentence, introduce a few sentences of your own, describing the man and the two girls going down the stairs and passing through the exit doors into the street. Details about sounds, as well as visual details, might help to make your description vivid. (To make it join up better with Lawrence's imagine that his sentence ends at *stairs* and that he didn't write *to the street*).

11 Make up three sentences, with active verbs, which could be changed into the passive form. For this to be possible the verbs must be used transitively. Then hand what you have written to your neighbour for him to rewrite the sentences in the passive.

23   A noun in apposition

A noun may be placed near another noun in such a way as to show that it is the same person, or the same thing, seen from a different point of view or in more detail.

The comedian, a small man with a big black moustache, hardly raised any laughs at all.

Man is placed beside *comedian,* and it is the same person. When a noun is identified in that way with another noun, by being placed near it, it is said to be in apposition to it. *Man* is in apposition to *comedian.*

'It's a nasty night,' he said. 'Shall you come and have a drink of something – a cup of coffee – it's early yet.'

'Oh I don't think so,' she said, looking away into the night.

'I wish you would,' he said, putting himself as it were at her mercy. There was a moment's pause.

'Come to Rollins?' he said.

'No – not there.'

'To Carson's then?'

There was a silence. The other girl hung on.

'Will your friend come as well?'

There was another moment of silence, while the other girl felt her ground.

'No thanks,' she said. 'I've promised to meet a friend.'

'Another time, then?' he said.

'Oh, thanks,' she replied, very awkward.

'Good night,' he said.

'See you later,' said his girl to her friend.

'Where?' said the friend.

'You know, Gertie,' replied his girl.

'All right, Jennie.'

The friend was gone into the darkness. He turned with his girl to the tea-shop. He was looking at her all the time, perceiving her, appreciating her, finding her out, gratifying himself with her. He could see distinct attractions in her.

Her eyebrows, with their particular curve, gave him keen
aesthetic pleasure.

---

1 In conversation we often miss words out. *See your later*. What two
  words did Jennie miss out? And what kind of word is each one?

2 At what point in the conversation, do you think, did the man first
  know for certain that the girl would come with him? Explain why
  he would have known.

3 Write down three nouns naming three different kinds of feeling
  that Gertie might have had, simultaneously, during those
  moments.

4 *This week's programme, a mixture of comedy and melodrama, did not
  appeal to him.* Which noun is in apposition in that sentence, and
  which noun is it in apposition to?

5 *. . . perceiving her, appreciating her, gratifying himself with her.* What
  nouns can be derived from those three verbs?

6 Which is the finite verb in the third sentence of the last paragraph?

7 Turn *distinct* (in the last sentence but one) into a noun by adding a
  suffix. Then, by adding a different one, turn it into an adjective.

8 What does *aesthetic* mean (in the last sentence)? Guess its meaning
  from the context if you don't know it, and then look in a
  dictionary.

9 *The colour —— in her cheek.* Complete the sentence by putting in
  the finite verb. Then look at the extract on page 48.

10 Picture Carson's tea-shop, and in a short paragraph describe it,
  mentioning where they sat.

24 A noun as the indirect object of a verb

Sometimes a noun has a *to* concealed in front of it.

The girl handed the doorman a key.

A *to* is concealed in front of *doorman.* It must be, because *doorman* is quite clearly not the object of *handed:* the girl didn't hand the doorman – she handed the key. And she handed it *to* the doorman. A noun with a *to* hidden in front of it like that is called the indirect object of the verb. *Doorman* is the indirect object of *handed.*

'Shall we go, then?' he said.

She rose in silence, as if acting without a mind, merely physically. He seemed to hold her in his will. Outside it was still raining.

'Let's have a walk,' he said. 'I don't mind the rain, do you?'

'No, I don't mind it,' she said.

They turned into the dark streets. He held her umbrella over her, and put his arm round her. She walked as if she were unaware. But gradually, as he walked, he drew her a little closer, into the movement of his side and hip. She fitted in there very well. It was a real good fit, to walk with her like this. It made him exquisitely aware of his own muscular self.

He led her into the park, where it was almost dark. He noticed a corner between two walls, under a great overhanging bush of ivy.

'Let us stand here a minute,' he said.

---

1 *Her eyebrows gave him ——— aesthetic pleasure. Great* is an adjective that would fit in there, but it is very general. Try to think of a more sharply focussed one, and then turn back to the last sentence of the extract on page 51.

2 In the fifth paragraph Lawrence introduces one piece of 'incorrect' grammar. Quote it, and explain where the incorrectness lies.

3 The 'incorrectness' adds life to the passage. In what way?

4 *He led her into the park . . . He gave her a smile . . . He told her his name . . . He drew her closer . . . He showed her the lake.* Every *her* is either the object of the verb or the indirect object of it. Look at each one in turn, and write either 'obj.' or 'ind. obj.'

5 By adding a suffix turn *will* (line 3) into an adjective meaning *having a strong will.* Be careful over the spelling.

6 What other noun in the same paragraph could we turn into an adjective by adding the same suffix?

7 *Outside,* in line 3, is an adverb. Make up a sentence in which it's a noun, and another one in which it's an adjective.

8 What kind of word is *overhanging* (in the last line but one)?

9 Turn *muscular* (line 14) into a noun by shortening it; and then into another one by lengthening it.

10 *He noticed a corner.* What adjective – meaning *easily noticed* – corresponds to the verb *to notice?*

11 *'Let us stand here a minute,' he said.* In two or three sentences describe the sounds those two might have heard, from the park and the city, as they stood there under the ivy-bush in the rain.

25 A noun as the complement of a verb

He consulted a lawyer.

Lawyer completes the sentence – by standing as the object of *consulted*.

He was a lawyer.

Lawyer completes that sentence too, but not by standing as the object of *was*. *Was* is not transitive. You can't *was* anybody. *Lawyer* completes the sense of *was* by repeating the subject in a different form. *He* and *lawyer* are the same person. *Complement* means *completion,* and a noun that completes the sense of a verb in the way that *lawyer* does there, is called the complement of the verb.

'Don't,' she cried, and she flung her hand across and hit him violently. 'Keep off of me.'

'Why, what's the matter?' he said, with suave irony. 'Nobody's going to hurt you.'

'I know what *you* want,' she said. 'Well, you're not going to have it off *me*.'

'Aren't I? Well then I'm not. It's no use crying about it, is it?'

'No, it isn't,' said the girl, rather disconcerted by his irony.

'But there's no need to have a row about it. We can kiss good night just the same, can't we?'

She was silent in the darkness.

'Are you a married man?' she asked at length.

'What if I am?' he said.

She did not answer.

'I don't ask whether *you're* married or not,' he said.

'You know jolly well I'm *not*,' she answered hotly.

'Shall I see you next week – next Saturday?' he said, as they returned to the town. She did not answer.

'Come to the Empire with me – you and Gertie,' he said.

'I should look well, going with a married man,' she said.

'I'm no less of a man for being married, am I?'

'Oh, it's a different matter altogether with a married man,' she said, in a ready-made speech.

So he left her. He did not know her name. He caught a train and went home.

What two adverbs in that passage suggest that the girl had a quick temper?

What extra word did the girl put in, in one expression, that a more educated person would not have included? What kind of word is it?

. . . *he said, with suave irony* (line 3). Look in a dictionary to see what those two words mean, and then, without using either of them, describe his tone of voice.

Hurt, in line 4, is a verb. Can you turn it into an adjective by adding a suffix?

What kind of word is *disconcerted*, in line 9, and what noun does it modify?

I should look well, going with a married man. What kind of word is *going*, and what word does it modify?

In the extract on page 48, in the fourth paragraph, there are two nouns standing as complements to verbs. Which are they?

Write down all the finite verbs in the last paragraph, and after each one either write *transitive* and quote the noun that is the object of the verb, or else write *intransitive*.

'Come to the Empire with me – you and Gertie,' he said. What adverb could be fitted in after *said*, as an extra, to tell the reader what tone of voice the man used?

Why do you think he added *you and Gertie*?

'Oh, it's a different matter altogether with a married man,' she said, in a ready-made speech. What does *ready-made* tell us about the speech, and about the way she spoke those words?

Sentences

Extracts taken from

Nevil Shute:
A Town Like Alice

A clause is a group of words that includes a finite verb: *The sun came out.* That is a clause. *When the sun came out* . . . So is that.

The difference between them is a simple one. *The sun came out* can stand on its own because it is a complete statement: *when the sun came out* can't, because it merely provides a *setting* for a statement. The first one is a main clause; the second, a subordinate one.

A subordinate clause, being incomplete, must always attach itself to a main clause – to the clause which completes the statement:

When the sun came out the heat was intense.

Subordinate clauses usually hang on an introductory word – on a word like *when* or *because* or *although* or *that* or *while* or *if.* These words are called subordinating conjunctions, because they join subordinate clauses to main clauses.

The extracts that follow come from A Town Like Alice, *by Nevil Shute. The party of prisoners consisted of thirty-two women and children. They were being held in the accounts office of a small Malayan town.*

Gradually they grew accustomed to their hardships. It was explained to them by Captain Yoniata that the victorious Japanese had no time to construct prison camps for women. When all Malaya had been conquered they would be moved into a commodious and beautiful camp in the Cameron Highlands, a noted health resort up in the hills. There they would find beds and mosquito nets. But to earn these delights they must do good things. Doing good things meant getting up and bowing whenever he approached. After a few shins had been kicked by Captain Yoniata's army boots, they learned to do this good thing.

There are seven sentences in that passage, separated from each other by full stops. They can be described like this: 'First sentence: a main clause only. Second sentence: a main clause followed by a subordinate clause.' Will you now describe the remaining five in the same way.

2 *At the end of the war they would be moved into a beautiful camp. There they would have beds and mosquito nets.* By using *where* join those two sentences into a single one consisting of a main clause followed by a subordinate clause.

3 *Some of the children remained quite healthy in spite of the bad food.* That sentence consists of a main clause only. By using *although* turn it into a sentence containing a subordinate clause as well.

4 The verbs on which main clauses are centred are called main verbs. Which is the main verb in the last sentence but one? And in the last sentence?

5 From one of the other sentences quote a main verb which is in the passive. And then quote a passive verb that comes in a subordinate clause.

6 *Beautiful,* in line 5, is an adjective. How many different words can you turn it into either by taking away suffixes or by adding them? First write down the word you have thought of, then the name of the kind of word it is, and then make up a sentence in which it is used as that kind of word.

7 What kind of word is *health* in line 6? And what part is it playing here? If you find it difficult to decide turn to question 4 on page 5.

8 Can you find three more words in the passage which are playing the same part?

9 What words in this passage seem to be the exact words used by Captain Yoniata?

27 'And', 'but', and 'or'

These words join like to like. It may be a noun to a noun (*women and children*), an adverb to an adverb (*quickly but steadily*), or an adjective to an adjective (*either hot or cold*).

The path through this part of the jungle was clearly marked, and they had no difficulty in finding their way.

In that sentence the *and* joins two main clauses together. This is a very common and useful way of constructing a sentence. We often use it when there is a close kinship between the clauses.

But, too, is often used to join main clauses together:

The children soon learnt to sleep on the floor, but the adults never got used to it.

Because they join like things to like things, *and, but,* and *or* are called co-ordinating conjunctions.

They received no medical attention and no drugs whatsoever. At the end of the week dysentery attacked them, and the nights were made hideous by screaming children stumbling with their mothers to the latrine. Malaria was always in the background. To check the dysentery Captain Yoniata reduced the soup and increased the rice ration, adding to the rice some of the dried, putrescent fish that had formerly made the soup. Later, he added to the diet a bucket of tea in the afternoon, as a concession to English manners.

Through all this time, Jean shared with Mrs Holland the care of the three Holland children. She suffered a great deal from weakness and a feeling of lassitude, but she slept soundly. Eileen Holland suffered much more. She was older, and could not sleep so readily upon the floor, and she had lost much of the resilience of her youth. She lost weight rapidly.

---

1   Will you now make a list of all the main verbs in that passage –
that is to say, all the finite verbs which belong to main clauses
(not those that belong to subordinate clauses) – and whenever
they are joined by an *and* or a *but* join them with an *and* or a *but* in
your list.

2   Quote in full the one subordinate clause in the passage.

3   *The prisoners always listened in silence when Captain Yoniata spoke. If
they interrupted him he was liable to kick them.* By using *because* join
those two sentences into a single one.

4   The sentence you have written has two subordinate clauses in it.
One is subordinate to the other: it is a subordinate clause *within* a
subordinate clause. Quote this 'inner' subordinate clause.

5   What kind of noun is *lassitude* (line 13)? How many other nouns of
this kind can you think of that end with the same four letters?

6   Which three words are the subject, the verb, and the object in the
last sentence of the first paragraph?

7   From what verb is the noun *concession* (line 10) formed? By
altering its prefix turn *concession* into as many different nouns as
you can think of. Then make up sentences in which they are used.

8   What kind of word is *adding* in line 7, and what noun does it
modify? (What noun is doing the adding?)

9   Will you now look back to question 7 on page 59, in which you
decided what grammatical part *health* was playing. Can you find
two words in the first paragraph of this extract which are playing
the same part?

10   One verb in this extract is in the passive form. Rewrite the clause
in which it occurs in such a way that it is used actively.

28 'And' used badly

We must be careful not to use an *and* to join together main clauses which are *not* closely related, and which should have a full stop between them. Doing this produces some very odd effects of speeded-up English. In a sentence like this next one, for example, it creates an impression of such breathless haste that one wonders if the writer hasn't knocked himself out:

The life of Lord Byron, the poet, who was a man of action as well, is one of the most exciting life stories I have read and after many romantic adventures and love affairs he died fighting for the Greeks at Missolonghi.

Here is one more example:

The greatest difficulty the mountaineers had to overcome was rounding the corner of rock on the north side and it took them two hours.

On the thirty-fifth day, Esme Harrison died.

Esme was a child of eight. She had had dysentery for some time and was growing very thin and weak. She slept little and cried a great deal. Presently she got fever, and for two days ran a temperature of a hundred and four as the malaria rose in her. Mrs Horsefall told Captain Yoniata that the child must see a doctor and go to hospital. He said he was very sorry, but there was no hospital. He would try and get a doctor, but the doctors were all fighting with the victorious army of the Emperor. That evening Esme entered on a series of convulsions, and shortly before dawn she died.

She was buried that morning in the Moslem cemetery behind the village. Her mother and one other woman were allowed to attend the burial. They read a little of the service out of a prayer book before the uncomprehending soldiers and Malays, and then it was over. Life went on as before in the accounts office, but the children now had nightmares of death to follow them to sleep.

She had had dysentery. What kind of verb is the first *had?* And what part of the verb is the second one?

Turn *convulsions* into an adjective. And *nightmare*.

Will you now make a list of the main verbs in the second paragraph, and whenever they are joined by an *and* or a *but* join them with an *and* or a *but* in your list.

Two of them are in the passive. Which two?

What word in the last paragraph is used in both its verb-form and its noun-form?

What do Captain Yoniata's replies to Mrs Horsefall reveal of his character and outlook? Try to introduce into your answer some carefully judged adjectives.

What does the pronoun *it* stand for in the last sentence but one?

What kind of word is *before* in the last sentence of the first paragraph? Make up a sentence in which it is a different kind of word.

The author's art is to make it seem that he is telling only the facts and never allowing his emotions to colour them, however sad the events may be. What do you feel is the result? Plain, factual reportage? Or is a sense of sadness conveyed, indirectly? Give reasons for what you say.

The obvious thing to have written would have been: *They read the service out of a prayer book*. But the author wrote: *They read a little of the service out of a prayer book*. Why do you think he added *a little?*

What use does Nevil Shute make of adjectives in this passage? Does he use a great many? Or very few? Are they original? Striking? Simple? Ordinary? In your answer refer closely to the passage and quote examples, and then go on to draw a brief conclusion about his style.

A sentence is a group of words which includes a main clause. Here are three sentences:

It was an afternoon in early autumn. The sky shone clear and blue after a misty morning. In the east a pale ghost of a moon was just beginning to rise.

An afternoon in early autumn. The sky shining clear and blue after a misty morning. In the east a pale ghost of a moon just beginning to rise.

In that second passage all the sentences are incomplete. The finite verbs have been left out in order to create the effect of a scene being sketched in a few swift strokes.

Doing that is a perfectly sound technical device. But it's a different matter when a person writes incomplete sentences not to achieve some special effect, but because he has allowed the easy-going habits of everyday speech to take over his writing:

The house was in a bad condition. All kinds of things wrong with it.

If you have a dog you need never be lonely. Because this animal makes the best friend a man could wish for.

People of this kind often take up dangerous sports. Like mountaineering or hang-gliding.

Will you now make those sentences complete – by putting in the missing finite verb in the first example, by re-uniting the subordinate clause with its main clause in the second one, and by punctuating the third one properly, so as not to chop a single sentence in two.

At the end of six weeks Captain Yoniata faced them after the morning inspection. The women stood worn and draggled in the shade of the veranda facing him, holding the children by the hand. Many of the adults, and most of the children, by that time were thin and ill.

He said, 'Ladies, the Imperial Japanese Army has entered Singapore, and all Malaya is free. Now camps are being built for men and also for womans and childs. Camps are at Singapore and you go there. I am very sad your life here has been uncomfortable, but now will be better. Tomorrow you start to Kuala Lumpur, not more than you can go each day. From Kuala Lumpur you go by train to Singapore, I think. In Singapore you will be very happy. Thank you.'

Will you now rewrite the following passage in such a way that all the sentences are complete. Run some of them together if you think it improves the flow of the English: *The conditions that night were appalling. No mosquito nets. No beds. The night passed without a moment's peace. The children moaning and wailing fretfully for hour after hour, preventing the adults from sleeping. Towards dawn Jean dozed a little and then woke up with a start. Just in time to witness an intense mosquito attack. The one that comes with the first light of the dawn.*

Write out correctly the two words that Captain Yoniata got wrong in his second sentence, and explain why he made a mistake of that kind.

In a later sentence he got a preposition wrong. What preposition should he have used?

Faced, in the first sentence, is used transitively. Make up a sentence in which it is used intransitively.

What kind of word is *morning* in line 2, and what part is it playing in this sentence?

Adult, in line 4, is a noun meaning a *grown up person.* By altering it from the second syllable onwards and lengthening it, turn it into a noun that means a *person who is growing up.*

Putrid means *rotten.* By altering its ending turn it into a word that means *going rotten.* (It comes in the extract on page 60.) *Obsolete* means *out of date.* Turn it into a word that means *going out of date.*

Captain Yoniata's words are created so vividly that we seem to hear him speaking them. How did he speak them? What did his voice sound like?

Write a short speech, spoken by Captain Yoniata in his characteristic manner. (He might perhaps thank the 'ladies' for having behaved well during their six weeks under his charge, and warn them to behave well on the march to Kuala Lumpur . . . and so on.)

Commas are the weakest kind of punctuation mark. They can only show where sentences pause, not where they end.

They were forced to march for nearly an hour through the rubber plantations, it made some of the older women very ill.

There are two sentences there because there are two main clauses. The writer should have put a full stop, not a comma, at the end of the first one:

They were forced to march for nearly an hour through the rubber plantations. It made some of the older women very ill.

Or else, if he had wanted to, he could have left the comma there and joined the two main clauses together with an *and*:

They were forced to march for nearly an hour through the rubber plantations, and it made some of the older women very ill.

From Panong to Kuala Lumpur is forty-seven miles. It took a minute for his meaning to sink in, then Mrs Horsefall said, 'How are we to travel to Kuala Lumpur? Will there be a truck?'

He said, 'Very sorry, no truck. You walk, easy journeys, not more than you can go each day. Japanese soldier help you.'

She said, 'We can't walk, with these children. We *must* have a truck.'

These were bad thoughts, and his eyes hardened. 'You walk,' he repeated.

For the remainder of the day they sat in stunned desperation. Those who had luggage sorted hopelessly through their things, trying to make packs which would hold the essentials and yet which would not be too heavy. Mrs Horsefall, who had been a schoolmistress in her time and had assumed the position of leader, moved among them, helping and advising. Mrs Horsefall had one child herself, a boy of ten called John.

___

1   I replaced one of the author's full stops with a comma. Which one? And why is a comma wrong?

2   What kind of word is *through* in the second sentence of the last paragraph? Make up a sentence in which it is a different kind of word.

3   Can you think of an expression in which *through* is an adjective?

4   *Hopelessly* is an adverb. See how many different words you can turn it into by giving the basic word different suffixes (but don't give it a prefix). First write down the word you have thought of, and then the name of the kind of word it is.

5   What kind of word is *trying,* in the second sentence of the last paragraph? And what pronoun does it modify?

6   *Essentials.* By shortening this word and altering its ending turn it into an abstract noun, and then make up a sentence in which this noun is used.

7   *Helping* and *advising,* in the last sentence but one, are participles. Make up two sentences (one for each) in which they are gerunds.

8   *Advising.* Write down the infinitive of this verb. Then form an adjective from it. And then write the noun.

9   Which is the main verb of the second sentence of the last paragraph? And of the sentence after that?

10 Which noun in the passage is in apposition? And which noun is it in apposition to?

11 I took out a pronoun and put in its place the noun it stood for. What pronoun? And from which sentence?

12 Describe Mrs Horsefall's character, in a short paragraph. We had another glimpse of her in an earlier extract, on page 62.

A full stop is not the only punctuation mark that can end a sentence. A semicolon can. It ends a sentence more gently than a full stop does, dividing it less sharply from the one that comes next:

They were forced to march for nearly an hour through the rubber plantations; it made some of the older women very ill.

So can a colon.

A colon ends a sentence in a forward-looking way. It tells a reader that in the next sentence the writer is going to explain what he has just said, or complete the sense of it. It tells him, therefore, not to lower his voice right down, as he would for a full stop, but to keep it half raised, expectantly:

In one respect they were better off in this camp: there was a doctor in attendance.

He had not risen to the post of Commander-in-chief through any military skill: he had bought his way up.

But this little community of villagers had been attacked by another enemy: cholera had reduced their numbers by nearly a third.

Jean and Mrs Holland had less of a problem: having lost their luggage they had less to start with and the problem of selection did not arise. They had few clothes to change into, and what they had could easily go into Jean's haversack. They had acquired two blankets and three food bowls between them, and three spoons, and a knife and fork; they decided to make a bundle of these small possessions in the blankets, and they had a piece of cord to tie the bundle with and to make a sling, so that one could carry the haversack and one the bundle. Their biggest problem was their shoes, which had once been fashionable and were quite unsuitable for marching in.

---

1   Why is there a colon between the first sentence and the second
    one?

2   After which word in the extract would a full stop have been just
    as acceptable as the author's punctuation mark?

3   *And* is used in that extract to join together, in pairs, these different
    kinds of words: two concrete nouns, two proper nouns, two
    pronouns, two main verbs, two verbs belonging to subordinate
    clauses, and two infinitives. Quote, from the extract, an example
    of each pair. In each case write three words only, with the *and* as
    the middle one; but for the infinitives it will be five words since
    two *to*s will come into it.

4   By adding a suffix of either two or three syllables turn *problem*
    into an adjective.

5   There are seven *had*s in the passage. How many of them are
    auxiliary verbs?

6   Turn *selection* into an adjective by altering its suffix.

7   See how many different words you can turn *acquire* into by
    altering its ending and adding suffixes.

8   Make up two sentences about some aspect of the plight of those
    prisoners. Work them out in such a way that the second one
    explains or completes the sense of the first one, and put a colon
    between them.

9   In the last sentence what position does the noun *shoes* occupy in
    relation to the verb?

0   The author describes how Jean and Mrs Holland packed their
    possessions into a bundle and tied them up. Describe how
    somebody else, in different circumstances, made up a parcel or
    packed a case or did some similar job. Include at least one
    adjective amongst your nouns, and at least one adverb to show
    how the person did the tying up or packing.

We can put the main point of a sentence towards the beginning of it:

Esme Harrison died on the thirty-fifth day, shortly before dawn, just when it seemed that the malarial fever in her was beginning to abate.

Or we can put it towards the end:

On the thirty-fifth day, shortly before dawn, just when it seemed that the malarial fever in her was beginning to abate, Esme Harrison died.

The first kind of sentence is called a loose sentence, the second kind a suspended one; but their names aren't very important. What matters is to understand the difference of character between them. The first kind is more leisurely and easy-going and natural. The writer comes out with his main point straightaway and then adds whatever he feels like adding. The second kind is more literary – more 'constructed'. But what it loses in naturalness it gains in forcefulness. By delaying his main point to the end – by 'suspending' it – the writer builds up a sense of expectation in the minds of his readers, so that when he finally does come out with it the effect is all the stronger.

Rice came to them soon after dawn, and at about eight o'clock Captain Yoniata appeared with four soldiers, who were to be their guard upon the journey. 'Today you walk to Ayer Penchis,' he said. 'Fine day, easy journey.'

It took an hour to get the last child out of the latrine and get the women ready for the march. The guards squatted on their heels: it was a small matter to them when the march started. Finally Captain Yoniata appeared again, his eyes hard and angry. 'You walk now', he said. 'Womans remaining here are beaten, beaten very bad.'

There was nothing for it but to start. They formed into

a little group and walked down the tarmac road in the hot sun, seeking the shade of trees wherever they occurred.

Will you find a good example of a loose sentence, anywhere among these extracts from *A Town Like Alice*. Quote the first and last words of it (putting dots between them) and the number of the page.

. . . And now a good example of a suspended sentence.

Re-arrange the second part of the last sentence of this extract (the part after the *and*) in such a way as to make it end with a main clause – that is to say, in the suspended form. You need only alter the order of the words, none of the words themselves; but you may like to put in an extra *they*.

Will you now turn to the extract on page 68. The last sentence is loose in form. By re-arranging the order of the words, and changing *was* to *were*, turn it into a suspended sentence.

Many sentences are a mixture, tending in some parts towards being loose and in other parts towards being suspended. Will you now look at the last sentence but one of the extract on pages 66–7, and say which direction you think it leans in. Explain the reasoning behind your answer.

Why is there a colon between the second and third sentences of the middle paragraph?

. . . *his eyes hard and angry* – two simple but vivid adjectives. How many other adjectives can you think of that could be used to describe Captain Yoniata's eyes at that moment?

'*Womans remaining here are beaten, beaten very bad.*' said Captain Yoniata, and he made three different grammatical mistakes. Will you explain what they are.

In one sentence describe some dramatic incident (perhaps a man falling to his death), and shape your sentence in the suspended form so that it ends forcefully.

33 The different kinds of subordinate clauses

There are three kinds of subordinate clauses: adverb clauses, noun clauses, and adjective clauses.

Adverb clauses fit into sentences in much the same way as adverbs do. They usually modify a verb:

They stopped talking when Captain Yoniata appeared.

When Captain Yoniata appeared modifies the meaning of *stopped:* it tells us *when* they stopped. We could put an adverb in the same place: *They stopped talking immediately*.

Noun clauses fit into sentences in the same way as nouns do:

They asked him what they should do.

What they should do is the object of *asked*. We might have written: *They asked him a question.*

Adjective clauses modify nouns, just as adjectives do:

He was a man who never showed any mercy.

We might have written: *He was a merciless man.*

The women went very slowly, making halts whenever a mother and child retired into the bushes by the roadside. There was no question of walking for an hour and then resting: the dysentery saw to that. For those women and children who were not afflicted at the moment the journey became one of endless, wearisome waits by the roadside in the hot sun. Within the limits of their duty the Japanese soldiers were humane and helpful; before many hours had passed each was carrying a child.

Slowly the day wore on. The sergeant had told them at an early stage that there would be no food and no shelter for the party till they got to Ayer Penchis.

In that passage there are three adverb clauses, one adjective clause, and one noun clause. Will you quote, first, the two adverb clauses that come in the first paragraph.

Then quote the adjective clause, and say what word – or words – it modifies.

And then quote the noun clause.

This clause is the object of *told*: it is *what* the sergeant told them. In what relationship to *told* does *them* stand?

The noun clause you wrote down for question 3 contains, as part of itself, an inner subordinate clause. Quote this inner clause. What kind of clause is it?

Why is there a colon between the second and third sentences?

What kind of word is *one,* in line 6?

Will you now quote from the passage two gerunds that are joined by an *and.* Write down all three words.

The Japanese soldiers were *humane.* What is the difference in meaning between *humane* and *human?*

See how many different words you can turn *human* into – first by adding prefixes and then by adding suffixes. (But adding both at once – we will say – is not allowed; nor are hyphens; nor can you count different forms of the same word – such as plurals, or the different parts of a verb.) After each word write down the name of the kind of word it is.

Four different suffixes are used in this passage: one adverb-forming, the others adjective-forming. Write them down, putting a hyphen in front of them.

Now look at the middle one of the three adjective-forming suffixes (middle in order of appearance in the extract). How many more adjectives can you think of that end with this suffix?

Adverb clauses are introduced by words like *when, because, although, if, as, until, while, before, as soon as, since, in order that.*

Eileen Holland found the conditions harder to bear because she was an older woman.

The *because* clause modifies the meaning of the main clause by giving it a background of *reason why.*

Although she felt ill she struggled forward.

The *although* clause alters the meaning of *struggled forward* by putting it in the setting of an opposing circumstance.

Other adverb clauses modify the main verb, or the main clause, in other ways. Those that begin with a word like *when* or *while* or *until* put the main happening in a framework of time; *if* clauses hedge it round with conditions; *in order that* clauses tell us about its purpose.

Adverb clauses also modify adjectives and adverbs:

The smoke was so thick that no one could see anything . . . The smoke poured down so thickly that no one could see anything.

There, the adverb clause (*that no one could see anything*) tells us how thick, or how thickly. Adverbs do the same job: *very thick . . . extremely thickly.*

As the day went on they all began to suffer from their feet. Their shoes were quite unsuitable for walking long distances, and the heat of the tarmac swelled their feet so badly that before long many of them were limping . . .

They stumbled into Ayer Penchis at about six o'clock that evening, shortly before dark. This place housed the labour for a number of rubber plantations in the vicinity. The latex-processing plant of one stood near at hand and by it was a sort of palm thatch barn. It was empty now and the women were herded into this. They sank down wearily, in a stupor of fatigue.

There are two adverb clauses in the passage. One of them modifies a verb. Quote it, and say what verb it modifies.

The other one modifies an adverb. Which adverb?

Stood, in the second paragraph, is used intransitively. It usually is. Can you make up a sentence in which the verb *to stand* is used transitively?

In the second paragraph there are three nouns in a row. What are the relationships between them?

What verb in the extract is in the passive?

Re-arrange the first sentence of the second paragraph in such a way as to change it into a suspended sentence.

What verb corresponds to *stupor* (in the last sentence)? And what noun (a four-syllabled one) can be formed from this verb?

Turn the following sentence into an adverb clause which can be tacked on to the end of the last sentence of the extract: *The soldiers busied themselves preparing a bucket of tea.* Think out what is the best conjunction to introduce it, change the full stop at the end of the extract to a comma, and then write the sentence out in full.

What kind of word is *number* in line 7? Make up a sentence in which it is a different kind of word.

See how many different words you can turn *number* into by adding different suffixes and prefixes. Then see how many different words you can turn *numer-* into. After each word you find say what kind of word it is.

Make up a sentence about some small incident that might have taken place on the march. Write it in the loose form. Then describe the same incident, or a different one, in a sentence that is suspended in form.

35 Noun clauses

A noun clause behaves like a noun. It may be the subject of a verb:

What worried them most was the danger of malaria.

Or the object of one:

No one knew who was supposed to be in charge . . . They soon discovered where the prisoners were hiding . . . They did not know when he would arrive.

Or it may be introduced by a preposition:

They could never rely on what he told them.

The conjunction which introduces noun clauses most often is *that*:

They said that they were refugees.

It can be left out:

They said they were refugees.

With the last of the light Jean strolled outside and looked around. She approached the sergeant and asked if she might go into the village. He nodded: away from Captain Yoniata discipline was lax.

In the village she saw mangoes for sale, and bought a dozen. She went back to the barn and found that the soldiers had provided one small lamp with an open wick fed by coconut oil. She distributed her mangoes, and found they were a great success.

The barn was full of rats, which ran over them and round them all night through. In the morning it was found that several of the children had been bitten.

They woke aching in new places with the stiffness and fatigue of the day before; it did not seem possible that they could march again. The sergeant drove them on, this time the stage was to a place called Asahan.

There is one noun clause in the first paragraph. What conjunction introduces it? And what is its position in the sentence? (The subject of a verb? The object? Introduced by a preposition?)

There are two noun clauses in the second paragraph. Will you quote the first one, and explain what its position in the sentence is.

And now quote the other one. What conjunction could we put in to introduce it?

That they could march again (in the last paragraph) is a noun clause, and it is the subject of the verb *did seem.* Don't be put off by the *it,* which anticipates it and is in apposition to it. This is a trick of English usage which makes it possible to save the noun clause till the end. The structure is: *That they could march again did not seem possible.* There is another sentence in the extract which has exactly the same grammatical pattern. Will you rewrite it, leaving out the *it* and putting the noun clause, which is the subject, in front of the verb instead of after it. Never mind if it sounds unnatural.

There is only one other subordinate clause. Will you identify it by quoting the conjunction that introduces it. What kind of clause is it?

Why is there a colon between the last two sentences of the first paragraph? Write a complete sentence for your answer.

In one place I put a comma instead of the punctuation mark the author put. Where did I do this? Why is the comma wrong? What do you think would be the best punctuation mark to use there?

Add a few sentences of your own to the passage, to be fitted in as an extension of the third paragraph, describing one rat-bite that one child received, and explaining what the women did about it. Try to keep your description in key with the author's style of plain factual restraint, and try to include – as he often does – one or two telling details.

36   Adjective clauses

Adjective clauses are usually introduced by *who* or *whom* or *whose* or *which*. They describe nouns – or rather modify them – just as adjectives do.

The man who sold her the mangoes was Chinese.

The *who* clause tells us about the man in the same way as an adjective might have done. We might have said, *The tall man was Chinese.*

The village, which consisted of a small cluster of thatched barns, lay near the mouth of the river.

The *which* clause describes the village.

It was a shorter stage than the day before, and it needed to be, because they took as long getting to it. This time the delay was chiefly due to Mrs Collard. She was a heavy woman of about forty-five with two children, Harry and Ben, who were aged about ten and seven. She had suffered from both malaria and dysentery at Panong, and she was now very weak; she had to stop and rest every ten minutes.

By the afternoon her somewhat ruddy face had gone a mottled blue, and she was complaining constantly of pains in her chest. When they finally reached Asahan she was practically incapable of walking alone. Their accommodation was another rubber-curing barn. They half carried Mrs Collard into it and sat her up against the wall, for she said that lying down hurt her. Somebody went to fetch some water, and bathed her face, and she said, 'Thank you, dearie. Give some of that to Harry and Ben, there's a dear.' The woman took the children outside to wash them, and when she came back Mrs Collard had fallen over on her side, and was unconscious. Half an hour later she died.

That evening Jean got more fruit and some sweets for the children. The Malay woman who supplied the sweets refused to take money for them.

---

1 Which two nouns does the adjective clause in the first paragraph modify? What kind of nouns are they?

2 What noun does the adjective clause in the last paragraph modify?

3 What kind of subordinate clause is the one introduced by *because* in the first sentence? And what word, or small group of words, does it modify?

4 In the middle paragraph there is a conjunction which means almost exactly the same as *because*. Which word is this?

5 Quote a noun clause from the same paragraph. How does it fit into the sentence?

6 Quote the subordinate clause in the sentence in lines 17–19, and say what kind of clause it is, and which word (or words) it modifies.

7 What noun (of two syllables) corresponds to *practically* (line 11)? Turn the word you wrote down into a verb by altering one letter of it.

8 Can you think of any more pairs of words like that, where the noun is distinguished from the verb by the same difference in the spelling? Write the nouns first, then the verbs.

9 Turn *finally* (line 10) first into an adjective, then into a noun, and lastly into a verb.

10 What adjective used in connection with Mrs Collard makes us feel that her plight was worse, probably, on those marches, than that of many of the other women?

11 Find three words which in this passage are nouns but which in different contexts could be verbs. Write them on a slip of paper and hand it to your neighbour. His task will be to make up three sentences in which they are verbs.

Who, whom, whose, and *which* are subordinating
conjunctions, but when they introduce adjective clauses
they are called relative pronouns. They are given that name
then because when they do that job they act as pronouns as
well as conjunctions.

*Mrs Collard, who had suffered from malaria, was finding it more
and more difficult to keep up.*

The *who* stands in place of Mrs Collard, as a pronoun
might, and at the same time, acting as a conjunction, it
introduces a subordinate clause and relates her to it. It
makes her the subject of it.

*Suddenly the sergeant, whom everyone regarded as a mild sort of
man, began to shout angrily.*

The *whom* stands in place of the sergeant, and at the same
time it introduces a subordinate clause and makes him the
object of it. *Whom* is like *him;* but it is not the same kind of
word because subordinate clauses flow from it.

In the morning they buried Mrs Collard. There was no
burial ground at hand but the Malay headman showed them
where they could dig the grave, in a corner of the
compound, near a rubbish heap. The sergeant got two
coolies and they dug a shallow grave; they lowered Mrs
Collard into it covered by a blanket, and Mrs Horsefall read
a little out of the prayer book. Then they took away the
blanket because they could not spare it, and the earth was
filled in. Jean found a carpenter who nailed a little wooden
cross together for them, and refused payment. They wrote
JULIA COLLARD on it and the date of death with an
indelible pencil, hoping it would survive the rain.

---

1   Nevil Shute writes in such a way as to seem to be a mere reporter,
     dealing only in plain facts. But he is skilled in the art of selection.
     In this paragraph he unobtrusively slips in a number of factual
     details which create an undertone of pathos. What details are
     these?

2   What noun does *who,* in line 9, stand in place of? And does it
     make this noun the subject or the object of the clause it
     introduces?

3   . . . *where they could dig the grave* . . . (line 3). What kind of
     subordinate clause is that one, and how does it fit into the
     sentence?

4   *Lowered* is not the same part of the verb as *covered,* in lines 5 and 6.
     Explain how the two words differ from each other grammatically.

5   *Indelible* (in the last sentence) means *not able to be blotted out or
     effaced.* What word means *not able to be destroyed?* And *not able to be
     repressed?* And can you think of two words that mean *not able to be
     avoided?*

6   Will you now re-arrange just the *first* part of the sentence that
     begins at line 7 – the part that goes as far as the comma – in such a
     way as to change the form of it from loose to suspended. Notice
     that in certain cases (and this is one) it is quite all right to use a
     pronoun *before* you have mentioned the noun it stands for. You
     will need to use one more comma than the author used.

7   What kind of word is *hoping* in the last sentence, and which word
     does it modify?

8   Is the last sentence loose or suspended?

9   In a single complete sentence explain why the carpenter refused
     payment.

The barn, which was part of the rubber plantation, was damp and draughty.

Relative pronouns nearly always refer back to a noun. This noun is called the antecedent. *Antecedent* means *going before*. *Barn* is the antecedent of *which*.

The antecedent usually comes immediately next to the relative pronoun, so that there won't be any muddle over which word it is. But occasionally, as long as there's no confusion, a few words can be put in after it, before we get to the *who* or the *which*:

The officer on duty that evening, who soon came to be known as 'the Major', spoke no English.

Occasionally, too, when *which* is being used, there may be no noun at all for an antecedent.

He refused to allow them to have any medicine, which was equivalent to condemning them to die.

What does the *which* refer back to in that sentence? Certainly not to *medicine*. It refers back to the fact which has just been mentioned – the fact of his refusing.

Captain Yoniata turned up about midday, driving into Kuala Lumpur in the District Commissioner's car . . . He turned to the women. 'You not go to Kuala Lumpur. English destroy bridges, so railway to Singapore no good. You go to Port Swettenham now, and then ship to Singapore.'

There was a stunned silence. Then Mrs Horsefall asked, 'Is there going to be a truck?'

'Very sorry no truck. You walk slow; easy stages.'

'Captain Yoniata, please be reasonable. Many of us are quite unfit to walk any further.'

He said, 'Englishwomans have proud thoughts, always. Tomorrow you walk.' He got into his car and went away; that was the last they ever saw of him.

Mrs Holland said despairingly, 'I don't see why he shouldn't have known at Panong that the bridges were down, and not sent us to Kuala Lumpur at all. It makes one wonder if there'll be a ship when we get to Port Swettenham . . .'

There was nothing for it, and next morning they started on the road again . . .

You walk slow; easy stages. What grammatical mistake did Captain Yoniata make this time?

Will you now turn back to the extract on page 66 and write down all the relative pronouns that come in the last paragraph of it. After each one write down its antecedent.

Some verbal adjectives can be turned into adverbs by having a suffix added to them. Quote one from this passage that has been turned into one.

Pick out from the passage a verbal adjective that is being used like an ordinary adjective, immediately in front of the noun it modifies.

'I don't see . . .' said Mrs Holland, and she went on to complete her sentence by using three noun clauses. Identify the first one by quoting the conjunction it is introduced by and its finite verb.

The second one is a noun clause *within* that first one. Quote the whole of it.

'and . . . not sent us to Kuala Lumpur at all.' What four words did Mrs Holland miss out between the *and* and the *not* – quite naturally, since they are carried over from earlier in the sentence and don't need to be repeated? (The third one is two words run together.)

'It makes one wonder . . .' Mrs Holland continued, and she went on to complete her sentence by using two subordinate clauses. What kind is each one?

What kind of word is *one* (in that same sentence), and what word could be used instead of it?

Nevil Shute tells us that when Captain Yoniata turned up he was *driving into Kuala Lumpur.* Why do you think he added this detail?

39   Adjective clauses: commenting and defining

There are commenting adjective clauses and there are defining ones.

The officer, who was a short, stocky man, did his best to help them.

The one in that sentence is a commenting one. Is the writer using the adjective clause to tell us which officer he is talking about? No, he isn't. He is using it to add a comment – to include a piece of information which he is putting in as an extra. That is why it is enclosed between commas. Commenting clauses always are, to show that they are not part of the main drift of a sentence.

The officer who took over from him was not nearly so helpful.

That is a defining one. It tells us – or defines – which officer the writer means. It couldn't be left out because the sentence wouldn't make sense without it. So it is not shut away between commas. A defining clause never is. It is gathered up into the flow of the words around it.

In the middle of the afternoon Ben Collard, who was the younger son of Mrs Collard, trod on something while walking barefoot in the grass that bit him with poison fangs and got away. He said afterwards that it looked like a big beetle; possibly it was a scorpion. Mrs Horsefall took charge and laid Ben Collard on the ground and sucked the wound to draw the poison from it, but the foot swelled quickly and the inflammation travelled up the leg to the knee. It was obviously painful and he cried a great deal. Somebody had some permanganate crystals and someone else an old razor blade; with this they cut the wound open a little, in spite of the child's screams, and put in crystals and bound it up; then they applied hot fomentations.

That, in the first sentence, is equivalent to *which.* It comes a long way after its antecedent; and there is a quite different noun next to it. Is there a muddle? Or does Nevil Shute get away with it? Give your reasons.

Is the adjective clause introduced by the *that* a commenting one or a defining one?

Explain why the other adjective clause in that sentence is a commenting one.

I put a noun in place of one of the author's pronouns. What pronoun should be put back, and in which sentence?

By altering its last syllable and adding an extra one, turn *inflammation* into an adjective. Make up two sentences to illustrate the difference of meaning between this adjective and *inflammable.*

There is one noun clause. Quote it, and say what verb introduces it and whether it is the subject or the object of that verb.

One sentence consists of five main clauses. Will you write down its five main verbs, together with the co-ordinating conjunctions that link them (nine words, with dots between them).

This is a particularly nasty scene, and to achieve this effect Nevil Shute has selected a number of unpleasant but convincing details. Which single detail do you think contributes the most?

Make a list of all the verbs in the extract, whether finite or not, expressing them as infinitives and putting a *to* in front of each one. Several of them could, in different contexts, be nouns. Make up sentences (one for each word) in which they are.

40 'That' as a relative pronoun; the relative pronoun left out

When defining clauses are being used two variations often come in. One is using *that* as the relative pronoun instead of the ordinary one:

It was an experience that taught them a great deal.

The other one comes in when the relative pronoun is the object of the clause it introduces. Then, more often than not, it is left out:

It was an experience they never forgot.

Relative pronouns often come after prepositions:

This plan, to which they had given so much thought, ended up in disaster.

The preposition can be switched from the beginning of the clause to the end of it.

This plan, which they had given so much thought to . . .

When the relative pronoun is left out, as it often is if the clause is a defining one, the preposition is bound to come at the end:

The town they lived in (in which they lived) . . . The man they spoke to (to whom they spoke) . . .

They got to Klang that afternoon, and here there was an empty schoolhouse, the sergeant put them into this.
Presently an officer arrived, marching at the head of a guard of six soldiers. This officer, whom they came to know as Major Nemu, spoke good English. He said, 'Who are you people and what do you want here?'

Mrs Horsefall said, 'We are prisoners, from Panong, on our way to Singapore. Captain Yoniata sent us here under guard, to be put on a ship to Singapore.'

'There are no ships here,' he said. 'You should have stayed in Panong.'

---

1   Is the adjective clause in the first paragraph a commenting one or a defining one?

2   In one place I put a comma instead of the author's punctuation. Where? And why is it wrong?

3   What kind of word is *this,* in line 2?

4   Which words are the subject, the verb, and the object in the sentence beginning at line 4? Write down three words only.

5   *They got to Klang that afternoon, and here there was an empty schoolhouse.* Will you turn that sentence into one that consists of a main clause followed by a subordinate clause, by putting a subordinating conjunction instead of *and here.*

6   Join the last two sentences of the first paragraph into one by turning the main clause of the first sentence into an adjective clause. You will need to put in an *and* and a relative pronoun, and alter the full stop after *English* to a comma, and cross out the *He.*

7   What kind of word is *marching* in line 3, and which word does it modify?

8   In that sentence *marching* is used intransitively. Can you make up a sentence in which the verb *to march* is used transitively?

9   *Captain Yoniata sent us here.* Rewrite this sentence with the verb in the passive form.

0   What adverb would come in well after *he said,* in the last sentence but one?

41 Phrases

A group of words *within* a clause is called a phrase.

The women sank to the floor aching with fatigue, while the soldiers went outside and began to prepare the supper.

The main clause of that sentence has two phrases in it: *to the floor* and *aching with fatigue.* The subordinate clause has one: *to prepare the supper.*

There are adverb phrases, adjective phrases, and noun phrases. *To the floor* is an adverb phrase. It modifies *sank.* We could put an adverb in its place: *They sank down. Aching with fatigue* is an adjective phrase: it modifies *women* in the same way as an adjective might. *To prepare the supper* is a noun phrase. It's the object of *began.* We could put a noun there: *They began the task of preparing the supper.*

The women stared at him in blank despair. Mrs Horsefall summoned up her flagging energy again. 'May we see a doctor?' she asked. 'Some of us are very ill – one child especially. One woman died upon the way.'

'What did she die of?' Major Nemu asked quickly.

'Nothing infectious. She died of exhaustion.'

'I will send a doctor to examine you all. You will stay here for tonight, but you cannot stay for long.' He turned and walked back to the camp.

A Japanese doctor, very young, came to them within an hour; he had them all up one by one and examined them for infectious disease. Then he was about to take his departure, but they made him stay and look at little Ben Collard's leg. He ordered them to continue with the hot fomentations. When they asked if he could not be taken into hospital he shrugged his shoulders and said, 'I inquire.'

---

1   At one point Nevil Shute reveals the thought in Major Nemu's
     mind by means of just one adverb. What adverb? And what was
     the thought?

2   Quote from the first paragraph a phrase introduced by a
     preposition . . . Then, from a remark made by Major Nemu, one
     introduced by an infinitive.

3   Now turn to the extract on page 86 and quote from it an adjective
     phrase, introduced by a participle, which contains within itself
     three inner phrases introduced by prepositions.

4   And now turn to the extract on page 80 and quote an adjective
     phrase, introduced by a participle, which contains a noun clause as
     part of itself.

5   By adding or taking away suffixes, or by adding a prefix, turn
     infectious into an adverb, a noun, a verb, a verb meaning the
     opposite, and a noun meaning *something which destroys germs*.

6   What adjective means *not able to be exhausted?*

7   Identify the adverb clause in the last paragraph by quoting its first
     and last words and putting dots between them.

8   It contains an inner subordinate clause. Identify this clause. What
     kind of clause is it?

9   Why is it perfectly clear what noun the first *he* in the last sentence
     stands for, even though the same pronoun was used in the
     previous sentence – and is used again later on in this sentence – to
     stand for a different noun?

10   *'Nothing infectious.'* What thought – or thoughts – perhaps flashed
     through Mrs Horsefall's mind when she made that reply?

Acknowledgements

Grateful acknowledgement is made to the following for their kind permission to reprint copyright material:

D. H. Lawrence: From *The Rainbow*. Reprinted by permission of Laurence Pollinger Ltd., the Estate of the late Mrs. Frieda Lawrence, and William Heinemann Ltd., publishers.

George Orwell: From *Decline of the English Murder and Other Essays*. Reprinted by permission of A. M. Heath & Company Ltd. on behalf of Mrs. Sonia Brownell Orwell, and Martin Secker and Warburg Ltd., publishers.

Nevil Shute: From *A Town Like Alice*. Reprinted by permission of A. P. Watt & Son on behalf of The Estate of the Late Nevil Shute and William Heinemann Ltd., publishers.

Cecil Woodham-Smith: From *The Reason Why*. Reprinted by permission of Constable & Co. Ltd.